SCANDINAVIAN MODERN

SCANDINAVIAN MODERN

Magnus Englund & Chrystina Schmidt

photography by Andrew Wood

RYLAND PETERS & SMALL
LONDON • NEW YORK

First published in 2003
This revised edition published
in 2013 by Ryland Peters & Small
20-21 Jockey's Fields
London WC1R 4BW
and
519 Broadway, 5th Floor
New York, NY 10012
www.rylandpeters.com

10 9 8 7 6 5 4 3 2 1

ISBN 978-1-84975-434-7

A CIP record for this book is
available from the British Library
and the Library of Congress.

Printed and bound in China

SENIOR DESIGNER Paul Tilby
DESIGNER Maria Lee-Warren
EDITOR Annabel Morgan
LOCATION RESEARCH Chrystina
Schmidt and Claire Hector
PRODUCTION Toby Marshall
ART DIRECTOR Gabriella Le Grazie
PUBLISHING DIRECTOR
Alison Starling

CONTENTS

INTRODUCTION

Scandinavian modern design, as a style, first emerged between the First and Second World Wars but peaked in popularity in the 1950s and is in vogue again today. It includes objects designed in Denmark, Finland, Iceland, Norway and Sweden. Scandinavia is the geographical region around Scandia, the mountain ridge running along Norway and Sweden, a land mass that included Denmark before the ice age separated Denmark from the north. Most Scandinavians refer to this area as the Nordic region, rather than Scandinavia.

Until the end of the 19th century, the Nordic region was a poor agricultural backwater. For most Scandinavians, money was short and eking a living from the land was a struggle. As a result, homes and possessions were simple, spare and functional. This pared-down design ethos continued into the industrial era, which started later in Scandinavia than the rest of western Europe. Decorative objects were produced mainly for the small upper class, and were often based on patterns borrowed from France, Germany and Britain.

During the 1920s a new decorative style appeared in Sweden, an elegant combination of modern lines and simple yet traditional detailing that appealed to the developing middle class. The new style received international recognition and was labelled Swedish Grace. However, it was soon superseded by something altogether more radical. Also in the 1920s, young

left Closeness to nature is a recurring theme in Scandinavian architecture. Buildings often blend into the surrounding landscape, but sometimes the contrast between modern architecture and nature can be dramatic.

opposite All the Scandinavian countries have long coastlines and a multitude of lakes. The winters might be cold and dark, but the summers are warm and bright and the summer nights are long, encouraging relaxed alfresco living.

Scandinavian architects were amazed and excited by the modernist
style emerging in Germany and France, which was replacing
decorative detailing with designs based purely on function and
modern technology. When the Swedish architect Gunnar Asplund
designed the Stockholm Exhibition of 1930, he turned it into a
manifesto for the new style. The exhibition sent a shockwave through
the Nordic countries and established modernism (or functionalism, as
it was often referred to in northern Europe) as the order of the future.

From the 1930s onwards, the Social Democrats dominated
political life in Scandinavia and put into place a tax-funded welfare
state programme. Housing, schools, libraries and hospitals were built
at a rapid rate, giving Scandinavian architects and designers many
new opportunities. The design and layout of new houses, in particular
their kitchens and bathrooms, were standardized to improve function
and hygiene. The design of household items, such as tableware and
door furniture, was reassessed to improve quality and performance.

this page Organic shapes
and styles are characteristic
of Scandinavian design, and
reached a peak during the
1950s. These fluid, curvaceous
outlines were very different
to the modern designs of the
Bauhaus designers, which
employed square shapes and
hard lines, but Scandinavian
designers still remained true
to the idea of creating simple,
functional forms.

opposite above left Quality
of light is naturally a priority
in a region where the sun sets
in early afternoon during the
winter months. The arrival of
electric light opened up new
possibilities and spurred
designers on to create the
ultimate light source for
reading, eating and working.

right and below Fine carving and polishing of wood is a heritage that the Scandinavian countries share. The old farming culture survived in Scandinavia longer than in most of western Europe, and making houses, furniture and tools from wood was part of daily life. Furniture and other pieces by master woodturners and cabinetmakers point to this heritage.

The 1930s also saw modern Scandinavian design making a breakthrough on the international stage. The Finnish architect Alvar Aalto exhibited his furniture at Fortnum & Mason in London in 1933 and at the Museum of Modern Art (MoMA) in New York in 1938. He also designed the Finnish pavilion at the New York World Fair of 1939. The Swedish designer Bruno Mathsson's furniture was selected for the MoMA collection before the museum even opened. Meanwhile, the Danish company Louis Poulsen enjoyed tremendous success with Poul Henningsen's PH lamps.

After the rationing of the Second World War years, there was an enormous demand for consumer goods in the Scandinavian home market. Production was fuelled by a desperate need for export revenue to kickstart the Nordic economies, particularly in Finland, which had to pay off a large war debt to the Soviet Union. While Europe remained war-torn and economically crippled, the Americans adopted Scandinavian design as the style of preference for a new modern age. The prestigious Georg Jensen shop on Fifth Avenue was a centre for Scandinavian design in the United States. When the new United Nations headquarters was built in Manhattan, Scandinavian designers were responsible for much of the interior. Meanwhile, Scandinavian designers were also winning prestigious awards at exhibitions across the world.

During the late 1960s, a divide between industrial designers and designers as artists became apparent. The focus on individual designers was questioned by a new, more politically aware generation. What had happened to the notion of good design for everyone? Scandinavian industrial design remained successful, but decorative design began to fall into decline. Italy continued to turn out numerous innovative products, beside which Scandinavian designs looked dated. Glassworks, ceramic factories and textile companies all faced falling sales, and many went out of business. For the manufacturers who survived, the only option was to follow foreign trends, often with unsuccessful results.

It was not until the late 1980s that a new generation of designers emerged in Sweden. Names such as Thomas Eriksson, Pia Wallén, Björn Dahlström and Thomas Sandell began to receive international attention, and leading Italian manufacturers such as Cappellini invited Swedish designers to work for them. The result was an explosion of creativity that has put Scandinavia back on the design map. This rediscovery of a regional design identity has been assisted by the international revival of interest in mid-20th-century design classics, which to a large degree focuses on Scandinavian design.

above The warm and relaxed mix of different styles, materials and colours in Scandinavian homes is far removed from the usual perception of a pared-down, minimalist Scandinavian interior. Wooden floors are usually preferred, both in flats and houses, and timber production is a major industry throughout Scandinavia.

right To combine old and new often makes an interior more personal. But Scandinavian kitchens are seldom anything but modern throughout, and function as the engine room of the home. There is a strong focus on developing new productions for the domestic kitchen, whether it be glassware, cutlery or other utensils, which makes Scandinavian design companies working in this field an acclaimed international force.

this page Making the most of the available light is achieved with large windows, but the Scandinavian climate also calls for good insulation and effective heating. There are few houses that do not have double glazing, and many have triple glazing to conserve energy and the environment while saving heating costs. The practical, ethical and economical often come together in Scandinavian design.

ELEMENTS

WOOD

Wood has always played a starring role in Scandinavian design. Each country has its own favourite: the Danes use beech and the Swedes pine, while the Finns prefer birch.

Historically, buildings, furniture, tools and household utensils in Scandinavia were to a large degree crafted from wood. While plastic, steel and concrete briefly stole the show during the 1970s and 1980s, wood has now resumed centre stage in Scandinavian design and architecture, often in unusual or unexpected ways. The new Nordic Embassy complex in Berlin is an excellent example of the use of wood in contemporary architecture.

above Dense Finnish pine and birch forests surround a house built from the same woods. The façade is made from pine while the interior floors and ceilings are crafted from birch.

right The stairwell of Jyrki Tasa's house in Finland is clad with birch veneer. In undiluted functionalist thinking, the construction is true to its purpose: what you see is what you get.

Before the advent of mobile phones, timber production was the dominant industry in Finland, and wood remains close to the heart of Finnish culture and the Finnish people. Wood has always been a major influence on Finnish design, architecture and interiors, and continues to be so today. A quarter of all Finns have summer houses, and few of these are without wooden saunas. The multi-talented Finnish designer Tapio Wirkkala is perhaps best known for his work in glass, but he was a prolific designer in many other materials, including wood. His sculptural pieces created from layered laminated wood and his exquisite wooden tables and bowls were directly influenced by the densely forested Finnish landscape. Wirkkala's work in glass, steel, ceramic and plastic was also informed by nature and the elements, and many of his designs were first made as prototypes in wood.

Wood has a unique density and functions well as an insulator against cold. During the Second World War, the Finns used spun wood fibre as a replacement for cotton. Products such as blinds, rugs and upholstery textiles can all be fashioned from spun wood fibre mixed with cotton.

opposite above left These veneered tables by Tapio Wirkkala are a perfect example of his awareness of the decorative potential of pure wood.

opposite below left A soaped oak sideboard by Eva Lilja Löwenhielm and Anya Sebton.

left The arrival of the wood-veneer Series 7 chair in 1955 set a new standard for mass-produced furniture. This sideboard and table are also made from wood veneer. Like many town houses in Scandinavia, this one has hand-laid parquet flooring.

below left Mixed with cotton, wood fibres can be spun into fabric and used for a multitude of products, like these seating cubes and cushions by Woodnotes.

above right The Finnish textile designer Ritva Puotila has worked with wood fibres since the early 1960s, and her artworks can be found in many Finnish homes, institutions and corporate buildings.

Wood functions well as an insulator against cold. During the Second World War, the Finns used spun wood fibre as a replacement for cotton.

The Finnish designer Ritva Puotila has long been a pioneer in this field. During the last thirty years, she has created both spectacular art pieces and more practical household products from humble wood fibre for her company, Woodnotes.

When Alvar Aalto first encountered the tubular-steel furniture of the Bauhaus in the late 1920s, his reaction was to adapt the Bauhaus design principles to a manufacturing process that better fitted both the Finnish tradition and his own idea of functional furniture. Aalto's main challenge was to find a way of bending wood in the same way that the Bauhaus architects and designers bent steel. After much experimentation, Aalto developed a new technique using steam and heat to bend and mould wood – a technique that is still in use today. For Aalto, wood represented a more humane, sympathetic material for a better, more democratic world – it was a warm yet practical

above and right Alvar Aalto designed the Paimio chair in 1931–2 for a sanatorium in the Finnish village of Paimio. While comfortable, it forces the sitter to sit upright, thereby improving breathing. The holes in the back are to relieve the tension created by bending the wood – the same problem as Arne Jacobsen encountered when designing his Ant chair.

ALVAR AALTO 100 1898 1998

artek

material suitable for use in hospitals, schools and nurseries. His choice of wood as a material can be seen as a political statement, not just a functional choice.

At the same time as Aalto was experimenting with bending and moulding wood, the Swedish designer Bruno Mathsson was designing chairs using similar techniques but with a very different end result. Mathsson came from a long line of cabinetmakers and devoted his long career (from the 1930s to the 1980s) to designing chairs that aimed to maximize the sitter's comfort. Mathsson was a bold innovator who devoted much time to the study of how people actually sat, years before the word ergonomic was in common usage. Mathsson's furniture designs were a huge sales success and made him the most well-known and respected Swedish furniture designer of the 20th century.

When the world went wild about plastic in the 1950s, Scandinavian countries still continued to produce a huge number of wooden objects. Teak was the wood of choice, particularly in Denmark, for furniture and homewares, including items such as salad servers, ice buckets, trays, sculptures, toys and much more. The long and venerable tradition of fine cabinetmaking remained strong in Denmark and these traditional skills were combined with bold contemporary styles, resulting in high-quality hand-made Danish wood furniture that was was hugely successful in the 1950s. Designers such

this page Aalto furniture is still manufactured using a technique that was originally developed in the early 1930s. Pieces are made from a single piece of birch wood that has been sliced lengthwise then glued back together, locked in position, steamed and bent.

left Børge Mogensen's Spanish chair is one of his most characteristic designs. It was inspired by traditional Spanish furniture designs, which Mogensen was introduced to by Kaare Klint, his tutor at the Royal Academy of Fine Arts.

below left An easy chair model no. 2254 by Børge Mogensen from 1958, upholstered in fabric designed by Lis Ahlmann. The seat of the chair slides forward to allow the back to recline.

above right During the 1950s, Denmark produced a huge amount of high-quality and sophisticated domestic items fashioned from teak and other dark woods. This ice bucket was designed by Finn Juhl.

below right Between 1951 and 1954, Finn Juhl designed a series of wooden bowls for Kay Bojesen, a silversmith now most famous for his wooden monkey, which has become something of a national symbol in Denmark.

opposite above left Finn Juhl was a master of detail. His most intricate furniture, such as this chair from 1946, was built in collaboration with master cabinetmaker Niels Vodder.

opposite below left and right Side tables and drink trolleys were very much in vogue during the 1950s and '60s. On top of an Alvar Aalto trolley model no. 901 (left) sits an ice bucket from 1960 designed by Jens Quistgaard and manufactured by Dansk International. Dansk was an American company set up in the 1950s to produce and market Danish designs in the United States and Europe.

The ingenious use of different woods and various skilled joining techniques means that many Danish pieces from this era are works of art.

as Kaare Klint, Finn Juhl and Hans Wegner designed chairs that won awards around the world and made Danish furniture into a major industry. The ingenious use of different woods and various skilled joining techniques means that many Danish pieces from this era are works of art. Hans Wegner claimed that if a chair is still beautiful when turned upside down, then it is a good chair, and he applied this conviction to some 500 different designs. Many designs are still made today in small workshops across Denmark, some by the very same craftsmen who made them half a century ago.

During the 1940s, the American aeronautical engineering industry developed a new method of bending and moulding plywood. The technique was soon applied

to furniture design by the innovative American designers Charles and Ray Eames. In 1952, the Danish architect and designer Arne Jacobsen developed a stackable chair made from a single piece of plywood on a tubular steel base that was suitable for mass production. Jacobsen's biggest difficulty was eliminating the tension in the wood. As a result, he designed a chair with a very narrow waist, resembling the shape of an ant.

Jacobsen approached the established Danish furniture manufacturer Fritz Hansen, with whom he had previously worked, but they were cautious about committing themselves to the production of this strange new design. To get the project off the ground, Jacobsen placed an order for 300 chairs for the architectural project he was currently working on, convincing Fritz Hansen that it was worth investing in the necessary equipment to produce the chair. In 1955 another Jacobsen plywood chair, the Series 7, was launched. With a broader back and four steel legs, it offered increased comfort and stability, and soon became a standard for all stackable plywood tubular-steel-legged chairs. Available today in ash, beech, cherry, elm, maple, oak, pine and walnut, as well as dozens of lacquered colours, this chair remains the single most recognizable piece of modern Scandinavian furniture design.

below left The PK 0 chair by Poul Kjaerholm from 1952 is an unusual experiment in bent wood by a designer best known for working in steel, glass and marble. It was not put into production until 1997, when Fritz Hansen produced 600 numbered chairs.

below right The Wishbone Chair (known as the Y chair in Scandinavia) by Hans Wegner, dating from 1950, is his best-selling design. To this day, each individual chair is still signed by the craftsman who made it.

this page Arne Jacobsen's Series 7 chair is probably the single most recognizable piece of Scandinavian design. Since its introduction, copies have flooded the market, including the one used as a prop in the famous photograph of Christine Keeler. The main difference between copies and originals lies in the quality of the construction. Fritz Hansen, the original manufacturer, uses cotton sheets interlined between layers of laminate, which gives greater flexibility to the shell.

GLASS

The concept of art glass is relatively new to Scandinavian countries, where most of the important glassworks were still producing bottle and window glass up until the 1920s.

The starting point for the modern Scandinavian glass industry was the international success of the Swedish glassworks Orrefors, founded in 1898. With the arrival of the artists Simon Gate in 1917 and Edward Hald in 1918, a new era dawned at Orrefors. New techniques and styles were developed, and Orrefors won numerous awards at the Paris Exhibition of 1925 for its Swedish Grace-style vases. Orrefors' success continued up to and through the 1950s with designers like Ingeborg Lundin and Sven Palmqvist and with Gunnar Cyrén in the 1960s. Like so many other Scandinavian glassworks, Orrefors suffered a decline in the 1970s and, despite periods of recovery, the last glass was blown at the village of Orrefors in 2012, even though the brand lives on.

Traditionally, Orrefors' two main competitors were Kosta (founded in 1742) and Boda (founded in 1874).

opposite page This unique series of vases, named Kivi (Stone) for obvious reasons, were designed by Ritva Puotila at Hadeland glass works in Norway in 1989. She was working as an experimental glass designer and freelance designer for Hadeland at the time. Today the vases are on display in the home of her son, Mikko Puotila.

left Ann Wåhlström has worked for Kosta Boda in Sweden and bridges the gap between the studio glass tradition and the heritage of Swedish glass-making. On the left is a Soap Bubble vase, and on the right a vase that represents a unique experiment with colours.

below left The PK 61 table by Poul Kjærholm has a top made from a thick piece of toughened glass that reveals the intricate construction of the steel legs.

Finnish glass is very different from Swedish – less inviting and flirtatious, perhaps, but just as advanced and refined. Perhaps the best-known glass object in the world is the Savoy vase, designed by Alvar Aalto in 1936 and produced by the Finnish glassworks Iittala in the remote Finnish village of the same name.

Today Orrefors and Kosta Boda are owned by the same company, but the two firms retain their individual identities. From 1950, with Vicke Lindstrand as artistic director, Kosta enjoyed a strong period thanks to the designer Mona Morales-Schildt, while at Boda Erik Höglund and later Signe Persson-Melin redefined Swedish glass. While Orrefors prides itself on the purity of its glass, Kosta Boda has created a name for itself with richly coloured glassware by designers like Ulrica Hydman-Vallien. Recent designers at Kosta Boda include Gunnel Sahlin and Ann Wåhlström.

In the same region of southern Sweden as Orrefors and Kosta Boda (often referred to as 'glasriket' – the glass country) sits a string of smaller glassworks such as Pukeberg, Lindshammar, Skruf, Nybro, Bergdala and Åfors, some of them over a hundred years old. The Swedes are very proud of their glassmaking tradition, and visiting the glass country is a popular summer treat, offering an opportunity to see the glassblowers at work.

Finnish glass is very different from Swedish – less inviting and flirtatious, perhaps, but just as advanced and refined. Perhaps the best-known glass object in the world is the Savoy vase, designed by Alvar Aalto in 1936 and named after the Savoy restaurant in Helsinki and produced by the Finnish glassworks Iittala in the village

left First flowing, then frozen, the glassmaking process is reminiscent of the Scandinavian seascape. Here, decorative pieces from local glassworks are placed just where they can catch the light.

above The magic of handmade glass is that each piece is always slightly different. Inspired by melting ice at the end of winter, this Finnish glass is close to nature in both shape and colour.

of the same name. Iittala had a good designer in Göran Hongell, but with the arrival of Tapio Wirkkala and Kaj Franck in 1946, and Timo Sarpaneva in 1950, Iittala experienced a creative explosion. Sarpaneva and Wirkkala created an endless series of both art glass and utility pieces for Iittala. Other talented designers such as Saara Hopea at Nuutajärvi, and Helena Tynell and Nanny Still at Riihimäki developed Finnish glass still further and made glass the most internationally celebrated Finnish design of the era.

Glass is still a source of national pride in Finland, but art glass is no longer a priority at Iittala. Instead, the focus is on mass-produced domestic glassware.

Glass is still a source of national pride in Finland, but art glass production is no longer a priority at Iittala, which now owns Nuutajärvi. Instead, the focus is firmly on mass-produced glassware for domestic use. Classics such as Kaj Franck's 1950s Kartio series and Aino Aalto's 1930s Aino series have been reissued and are bestsellers once more, while contemporary designs by international names such as Konstantin Grcic and Alfredo Häberli continue Iittala's functionalist tradition.

this page The bark effect of this glass vase is typical of Timo Sarpaneva's work for Iittala during the 1960s. His later work is stricter in form.

right This pitcher by Kaj Franck from the Kartio series for Iittala was originally covered with rattan – highly decorative, but rather less practical once dishwashers were introduced.

opposite The Nappi (Button) tealight candle holders were designed by Markku Salo for Iittala in 1998. They are a good example of Iittala's affordable, mass-made but nonetheless well-designed glassware.

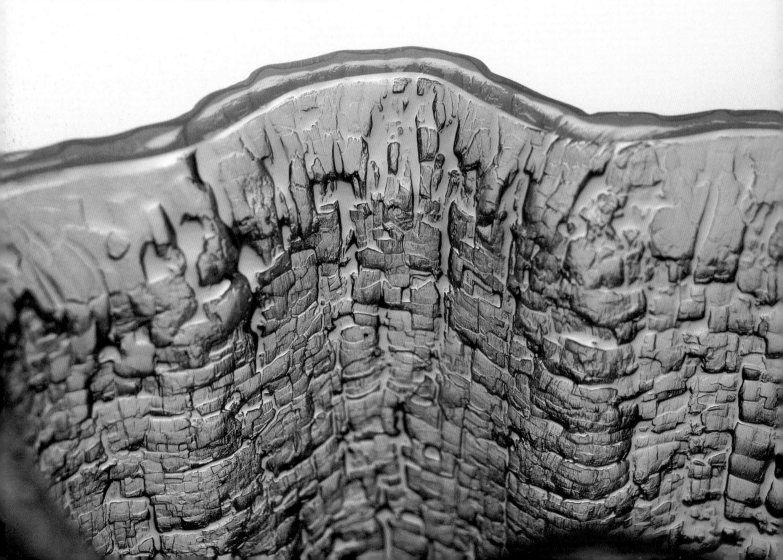

Some interesting glass is currently being produced at Riihimäki (home of the Finnish glass museum, created by Tapio Wirkkala) by independent designers such as Kristian Venäläinen and Pertti Metsälampi, but unfortunately it has limited distribution outside Finland.

The main glassworks in Denmark are Holmegaard and its now-defunct sister factory Kastrup. In 1942,

Holmegaard and Kastrup enjoyed great success with contemporary glass during the 1950s and employed some of the best Danish designers of the time – Henning Koppel, Grethe Meyer, Nanna and Jørgen Ditzel and Otto Brauer, to name but a few.

Holmegaard experienced a creative change with the arrival of a new artistic director, Per Lütken, whose numerous creations of the 1940s and 1950s are boldly organic and adventurously fluid in form. Both Holmegaard and Kastrup enjoyed great success with their contemporary glass during the 1950s and employed some of the best Danish designers of the time – Henning Koppel, Grethe Meyer, Nanna and Jørgen Ditzel and Otto Brauer, to name but a few. By the late 1960s Holmegaard had gone distinctly pop, and even launched a colourful range named Carnaby, but in 1979 the Kastrup factory closed down.

While vintage Holmegaard glass is now highly collectible, the current glass production is mainly aimed at the home and tourist markets. This is also true of Hadeland, the most prominent Norwegian glassworks, where the designer Arne Jon Jutrem was a strong name between 1950 and 1962.

opposite above Otto Brauer designed a series of large bottles while working at Holmegaard in the 1960s. Made in a multitude of colours, they are highly collectible today.

opposite below The Provence bowl, designed by Per Lütken in 1956 for Holmegaard, is still produced today. The bowl is made by pressing the hot mass of glass onto a wooden board soaked in water while quickly turning it, forcing the rapidly rising steam to create a cavity in the glass.

this page A glass vase and bowl by Per Lütken for Holmegaard share a table with a ceramic bowl by Stig Lindberg for Gustavsberg, Sweden. The freeform dish is typical of Lütken's organic shapes.

this page Curtains are often omitted when decorating Scandinavian houses, or are treated as a way of enhancing the light in a room rather than blocking it. Here, transparent linen panels are fixed to a track so they can be moved easily.

opposite Two Poul Kjærholm PK 22 chairs sit on a rug from IKEA designed by Eva Lilja Löwenhielm.

TEXTILES

The Scandinavians use textiles to bring warmth and interest to their interiors. Fabrics and rugs are a quick and inexpensive way of transforming a room.

Although Nordic fashion houses such as Denmark's Vera Moda and Sweden's H&M are internationally successful, very little clothing is manufactured in Scandinavia. However, many small but important textile manufacturers are dotted around the region, based around traditional, high-quality and labour-intensive workshop production. Their great advantage is that they are able to create small series of fabrics and experiment with colours and designs.

The work of Austrian architect Josef Frank bridges the gap between traditional and modern Nordic style and between international and Scandinavian design. Married to a Swede in 1911, Frank emigrated from Austria to Sweden in 1934 to escape the Nazis. Even though Frank took modernism as his starting point, his work was very different to that of the Bauhaus-influenced designers. He favoured natural materials such as cane and rattan, and curved forms instead of hard lines and right angles. As head designer for the company Svenskt Tenn and designer of the Swedish pavilion at the New York World Fair of 1939, Frank had a considerable influence. The upholstery and curtain textiles he created for Svenskt Tenn from the 1930s and 1940s are colourful and large-scale but at the same time amazingly detailed, often revealing strong Asian influences. Botanical motifs were his great passion. Many of Frank's textile and furniture designs are still in production today.

A master of form, line and composition, Märta Måås-Fjetterström is another central figure in Swedish textile design. She started her own weaving workshop in 1919 and continued to run it up until her death in 1941. A group of weavers has continued to realize Måås-Fjetterström's artistic intentions. For many years, Barbro Nilsson was the company's artistic leader, herself producing pieces that displayed a supreme mastery of technique and revealed a deep feeling for colour. Other artists have also regularly contributed new designs that are developed and produced by the talented in-house weavers. Today, fabrics and tapestries are still produced for clients across the world, and original Måås-Fjetterström work is highly priced at auction.

Since its opening in 1902, Nordiska Kompaniet (NK) has been the leading department store in Stockholm. Between 1937 and 1971, NK had its own textile manufacturing division. Astrid Sampe was head of the design studio, where she created a wealth of innovative printed and woven fabrics. She also employed numerous other talented designers, including Stig Lindberg, Sven Markelius, Viola Gråsten, Olle Baertling and Arne Jacobsen. Sampe also created rugs for the United Nations building in New York and was friendly with American designers such as Charles Eames, Eero Saarinen and Florence Knoll.

Possibly the most celebrated Scandinavian textile company is Marimekko, founded in Finland in 1951 by Armi and Viljo Ratia.

Although 10-Gruppen is not a large company, it has made a big impact, producing designs that have sold through IKEA, Habitat, Paul Smith and the Swedish Co-op. Thanks to a 40th-anniversary exhibition at the Swedish institute in Paris, 10-Gruppen has recently come back into focus.

Along with Nanna Ditzel, whose Hallingdal fabric for the company Kvadrat is a modern Danish classic, Vibeke Klint is the best-known Danish textile designer of the last 50 years. Klint designed rugs and mass-produced curtain and upholstery fabric. Her colourful abstract designs drew inspiration from India and the Klint textile history of traditional materials and techniques and simple patterns, which has dominated Danish textile design.

Ingrid Dessau, a contemporary of Sampe, designed rugs for the carpet manufacturer Kasthall between 1954 and 1978 and fabrics for Kinnasand from 1970 up until 1984. However, some of her most acclaimed work was produced in her own studio, including her herringbone- and goose-eye-patterned carpets and drapery of the 1950s as well as many other abstract handwoven pieces.

10-Gruppen (10 Swedish Designers) was formed in 1970 as a response to a creative and commercial crisis in the Swedish textile industry that stemmed from a lack of innovation and increased international competition. Most of the designers involved were already established names, but all shared the belief that the large textile companies did not appreciate the need for good modern design. 10-Gruppen's members included Inez Svensson, Ingela Håkansson, Gunilla Axén, Tom Hedqvist and Birgitta Hahn. 10-Gruppen's prints are bold and colourful.

above left Pia Wallén has returned to a simple cross shape in several of her designs, like this hand-tufted wool rug for Asplund. It can be interpreted as a symbol of positivity: a large plus sign.

right Wood fibres mixed with cotton make for a strong material, as in these Ritva Puotila cushions for Woodnotes. The fibres are so dense that little dust can settle into the fabric.

opposite This wood fibre rug by Ritva Puotila is a natural companion to the wooden furniture and shows that there are still ways of developing new products based on traditional Scandinavian manufacturing methods.

Her student Kim Naver developed Vibeke Klint's style still further with her work for Georg Jensen Damask, a Danish textile company (and no relation to the silvermaker).

Possibly the most celebrated Scandinavian textile company is Marimekko, founded in Finland in 1951 by Armi and Viljo Ratia. Marimekko's real breakthrough came with the 1960 US presidential election campaign between Kennedy and Nixon. Conservative newspapers had criticized Jacqueline Kennedy for her penchant for expensive French designer clothing, so when she bought some colourful and inexpensive Finnish cotton dresses from a shop in Cape Cod, the story was printed in some 200 newspapers across the country. As a result, Marimekko became an instant success story.

Somewhere between a company and a cult, Marimekko's mission was to produce colourful and comfortable clothing at affordable prices. It employed some of the most talented Finnish textile designers of its time, including Vuokko Nurmesniemi, Annika Rimala and Maija Isola. After a period of decline during the 1980s, Marimekko is now right back in fashion and reprinting many of its archive designs, such as Maija Isola's bold, iconic Unikko flower print from 1965, which has become something of a Marimekko trademark.

opposite and left These chairs for fashion company Vuokko by Antti Nurmesniemi are upholstered in a fabric by Vuokko Nurmesniemi. The striped Piccolo fabric she designed for Marimekko in 1953 was followed by Annika Rimala's Tasaraita stripe in 1968. The French might be regarded as the inventors of stripy tops, but thanks to Marimekko, the Finns have an even closer relationship to stripes – bedlinen, upholstery fabric, clothes, crockery and bags have all been produced in jaunty and colourful stripes. In 2001, the Finnish postal authority even released a Marimekko striped stamp. Jackie Kennedy wore cotton dresses by Vuokko Nurmesniemi in the early 1960s and Annika Rimala personally sold her a stripy knitwear shirt later in the decade. At one point, Levi Strauss & Co offered to produce Annika Rimala's stripy designs, but she politely declined.

below Maija Isola designed some of Marimekko's all-time classics, including the Kaivo fabric (top) and Unikko flower (bottom). Her large-scale designs in bold colours forced Marimekko to develop new printing techniques to match the large areas of colour. Several Maija Isola designs are in the permanent collection of the Museum of Modern Art (MoMA) in New York.

CERAMICS

The innovative glazes, colours and designs of modern Scandinavian ceramics means that they have few international competitors.

Some major changes have taken place in the Scandinavian ceramics industry during the course of the last 50 years, with several mergers and closures of many once-prominent manufacturers. Nowadays, notable ceramics are more often produced by independent designers working from small studios and are sold through galleries.

Danish ceramics are largely synonymous with two companies: Den Kongelige Porcelainsfabrik (the Royal Porcelain Factory), founded in Copenhagen in 1775, and Bing & Grøndahl, founded in 1853. In 1987 these two august old firms merged under the name Royal Copenhagen. During the first golden age of Danish ceramics in the 1880s, both companies developed a style that was inspired by Chinese porcelain but retained a distinctively Danish feel.

With the arrival of the functionalist style in the 1930s, Danish ceramics enjoyed a second golden era that continued until well after the Second World War, when Danish Modern became a byword for Scandinavian design. The celebrated designer Axel Salto was a key figure in Danish ceramics from the 1930s to the 1950s, along with other acclaimed designers such as Henning Koppel, Gertrud Vasegaard and Grethe Meyer.

Den Kongelige Porcelainsfabrik and Bing & Grøndahl never quite dominated Danish ceramics in the way that large manufacturers dominated the ceramic industries in Sweden and Finland. In Denmark there were also numerous small independent potteries producing

opposite Danish ceramics are produced and developed in small studios as well as by larger companies. These vases from 1997 were made by Bodil Manz in her own studio.

above left Stackability is a theme that several Scandinavian designers have returned to again and again, in glass, plastic and ceramics. These bowls are from Grethe Meyer's Blå Kant series.

below left These geometric dishes by Grethe Meyer are named Side By Side and were designed for Royal Copenhagen in 1996 but never put into production.

below right A pair of experimental pottery vessels by Finn Juhl stands on a windowsill in the home he shared with Hanne Wilhelm Hansen (see pages 82–87).

The 1930s to the 1960s was a golden period for Rörstrand and its two talented main designers, Gunnar Nylund and Carl-Harry Stålhane.

excellent work. Saxbo existed from 1930 to 1968 with the talented studio potters Nathalie Krebs and Eva Staehr-Nielsen in charge. The famous Kähler family produced pottery for four generations, from 1839 to 1969. Other notable firms included Palshus, Søholm, Holbaek, Humlebaek and Nymølle. Many of the smaller potteries developed a simple, rustic, handcrafted style that is still very sought after today.

The 1970s and 1980s were not a good period for Danish ceramics, due to growing international competition and fading interest in the Danish Modern style. Royal Copenhagen's response was to reissue a series of classic pieces dating from the 19th century. Nowadays, the best way to find interesting modern Danish ceramics is to visit the many small studios and workshops dotted across Denmark.

Founded in Stockholm in 1726, Rörstrand is Europe's second oldest ceramic factory. The 1930s to the 1960s was a golden period for Rörstrand and its two main designers, Gunnar Nylund and Carl-Harry Stålhane, who worked on both studio and production wares. With the decline in popularity of the Scandinavian Modern style in the 1970s, the design department was closed down, and in 1983 Rörstrand was bought by the Finnish company Designor. Production in Sweden ceased in 2005, even though the Rörstrand brand continues to live on.

above, from left to right
White vessels by Stig Lindberg and Gunnar Nylund; a bowl by Gunnar Nylund for Rörstrand; dishes and a vase by Stig Lindberg for Gustavsberg. The work of both designers has become increasingly sought after in recent years, not least in the United States, where mid-20th-century Swedish ceramics are highly appreciated.

right The Suomi (Finland) series was designed by Timo Sarpaneva in 1974 for the German company Rosenthal. It quickly became one of the company's best sellers and has been developed further with various colours and patterns. The pure white version is the one that does the Bauhaus-inspired design most justice.

opposite The Cirrus stoneware vase is designed by Pia Törnell and made at Rörstrand. It requires a mould with 13 different parts.

During the 20th century, Gustavsberg, the other leading Swedish ceramics manufacturer, employed perhaps the most interesting ceramic designers of the time, including Wilhelm Kåge, Stig Lindberg and Bernt Friberg. Founded in 1827, Gustavsberg is situated just outside of Stockholm on the Baltic Sea, where it received shipments of clay from England to manufacture its bone china. Owned by the Swedish Co-op from the 1930s, Gustavsberg began to produce porcelain sanitaryware and porcelain-enamelled steel for ovens and refrigerators. It also produced enamelled porcelain studio pieces. In the 1980s the factory was bought by Designor and closed down soon after.

Today, a small group of independent potters continue production at Gustavsberg, including the designer Ingegerd Råman. She also designs for Figgjo, a Norwegian company that has become the largest ceramic manufacturer in Scandinavia, supplying schools, hospitals and restaurants. Despite their focus on utility china, Figgjo also produced many interesting designs during the 1950s and 1960s and still maintains a high standard of design. The other leading Norwegian ceramics factory, Porsgrund, enjoyed great success with Nora Gulbrandsen as artistic director before the war and Tias Eckhoff during the 1950s. Nowadays the focus is on the domestic market.

With a 374-ft kiln – for a while the largest in the world – and over a thousand employees, the Finnish company Arabia was the biggest ceramic manufacturer in Europe during the late 1930s.

Finnish ceramics is dominated by Arabia, which was originally founded in 1873 as a subsidiary to Rörstrand but which has been under Finnish ownership since 1916. With a 374-ft kiln – for a while the largest in the world – and over a thousand employees, Arabia was the biggest ceramic manufacturer in Europe during the late 1930s. Although the company was a large-scale commercial manufacturer, the artistic director Kurt Ekholm set up an art department where some 30 artists were given the freedom to experiment without commercial constraints. In 1946, Kaj Franck took over as artistic director and surrounded himself with a number of other talented designers, including Ulla Procopé, Birger Kaipiainen, Oiva Toikka and Ulla Bryk, who was married to the designer Tapio Wirkkala (see page 27). Franck's Kilta series from 1953 (reissued as Teema in 1981) may well be the most famous Arabia product; its spare, simple lines encapsulating the essence of Scandinavian functionalism.

opposite The long, shallow decorated dish is typical of the playful designs Stig Lindberg produced for Gustavsberg.

left The Teema series by Kaj Franck was originally introduced under the name Kilta in 1953. The bottle with a cork stopper is a milk jug. Its base was designed to fit snugly between the inner and outer panes of a standard double-glazed Finnish window (in the 1950s both refrigerators and triple glazing were still unusual in Finland). In 1975, Arabia's new owners changed the factory's production from earthenware (which is not oven- or microwave-proof) to stoneware, and the earthenware Kilta series was discontinued, despite the fact that 25 million pieces had been sold. The outraged protests that followed made national news in Finland, and in 1981 the series was reintroduced in stoneware under the name Teema.

above These Gustavsberg pieces combine functional design with bold patterns.

this page This Arne Jacobsen teapot was produced by Stelton in 1967, part of Jacobsen's Cylinda Line. Creating this line required a monumental product development exercise on the part of Stelton's owner, Peter Holmblad (Arne Jacobsen's stepson). Details such as the non-drip lip and the seamless join between the spout and main body reveal the high level of finish and the perfection of each piece.

METAL

In Scandinavia, metal has been transformed into decorative objects since the time of the Vikings. Indeed, Viking silver, with its simple shapes and bold patterns, has had a huge influence on modern Scandinavian metalware.

The Danish firm Georg Jensen is one of the world's most famous silver manufacturers. Jensen himself retired in 1926, by which time the company employed hundreds of silversmiths (compared to some two dozen today). Early Jensen silver is of superb quality. The company enjoyed a second peak of popularity from the 1950s on, producing work by celebrated designers such as Henning Koppel, Jørgen and Nanna Ditzel, Bent Gabrielsen and Magnus Stephensen, all of whom also worked in steel. Henning Koppel's fish dish in silver has become something of an icon for modern Danish silversmiths. Georg Jensen's main competitor, A Michelsen, employed the architects Kay Fisker and Ib Lunding and originally produced Arne Jacobsen's steel cutlery for the SAS Royal Hotel, before Georg Jensen bought the company.

Unsurprisingly, given their skill with silver, the Danes are equally talented when it comes to working with stainless steel. Arne Jacobsen's Cylinda Line for Stelton dates from 1967. The pieces are made from large sheets of steel bent into cylindrical shapes and hand polished. The end result is a series of sleek, minimalist objects reminiscent of Bauhaus silverware. Stelton followed up the Cylinda Line with designs by Erik Magnussen, who created a simple but brilliant vacuum jug that is a standard feature in most Danish offices.

At the beginning of the 20th century, Swedish silver tended to be less decorative than that made in the Danish style, with some austerely beautiful jewellery, church decorations and cutlery being produced by Jacob Ängman and later Erik Fleming, Wiwen Nilsson and Sigvard Bernadotte. Sigurd Persson worked silver, gold and stones into modern styles and developed his shapes through his industrial designs for cutlery, pots, glasses and even such humble objects such as kitchen brushes. The popular jewellery designs of Vivianna Torun Bülow-Hübe are mainly associated with Georg Jensen, which still produces her classic steel bangle wristwatch from 1969, but the Swedish jewellery designer also had her own Stockholm studio in the 1950s before moving to France and later Asia.

The stainless-steel kitchenware produced by Finnish company Hackman (later branded as Iittala) in the late 1990s received much favourable attention. Designed by names such as Renzo Piano, Antonio Citterio and Björn Dahlström, Hackman's kitchenware set a new standard for cutlery, pans and kitchen utensils. The most celebrated Finnish

top Stelton developed several products with Erik Magnussen, such as this minimalist cutlery.

above Silver company Georg Jensen also produces stainless steel cutlery, like these spoons by Grethe Meyer.

silversmith of the past century is Bertel Gardberg, a master in silver, gold, brass and stainless steel as well as wood and glass. Gardberg's work can be found in many Finnish homes in the shape of the elegant Carelia cutlery he designed for Hackman. Gardberg's student, Börje Rajalin, has been the chief designer at the silver company Kalevala Koru since 1956, but he is also an industrial designer responsible for trains, ferries and even the Helsinki metro.

In the early 1960s, the Finnish sculptor and jewellery designer Björn Weckström's discovery of some gold nuggets in Lapland sparked a new style of jewellery design. A forerunner in his field, Weckström broke with traditional concepts of jewellery design by boldly combining different materials. Since 1963, Weckström has worked for the silver company Lapponia. Poul Havgaard, a Danish blacksmith and jewellery designer, began a long

During the 1950s and 1960s, Norwegian silver designers were among the most progressive in Scandinavia, particularly those linked to the company David-Andersen AS.

and fruitful association with Lapponia in 1971. Havgaard made his name in the 1960s, when he produced unique pieces of jewellery and sculptures forged from iron and steel. He still creates these pieces in his workshop on the island of Fyn in Denmark.

During the 1950s and 1960s, Norwegian silver designers were among the most progressive in Scandinavia, particularly those linked to the company David-Andersen AS. Harry Sørby joined the company in 1929 and designed for them right up to the 1970s, developing his style from classicism through functionalism into Scandinavian Modern. Norwegian silversmiths were innovative in their use of enamel, which was used to create almost psychedelic patterns by designers like Torbjørn Lie-Jørgensen and Uni David-Andersen. Another popular Norwegian innovation was cast silver, used by Unn Tangerud to make geometric-shaped pendants. Norwegian flatware was also a great export during the 1950s, not least the Maya cutlery series designed by Tias Eckhoff for Norsk Stålpress.

left Metal outdoor furniture designed by Antti Nurmesniemi stands on the terrace of Antti and Vuokko Nurmesniemi's home.

opposite above This lamp, model 1005, is Erik Magnussen's latest addition to a line of designs he has produced for the Danish company Stelton. Many of Magnussen's metal designs are developments or refinements of ideas he originally had when working

with ceramics for Bing & Grøndahl. Magnussen has also worked in silver for Georg Jensen and Selangor.

opposite The ship's lamp, model 1001 by Erik Magnussen, continues the minimal cylindrical theme for Stelton. The metal ring positioned around the glass can be manually adjusted to block out the glare of the flame and it has the added advantages of both heating and dehumidifying onboard.

this page The Formula chair is the latest in a long series of witty designs in plastic by the Finnish designer Eero Aarnio. As it is plastic, the chair can also be used outdoors. Note the space to hold drink cans in the side.

PLASTIC

The Italians enjoyed tremendous
success with plastics during the 1960s
and 1970s. Two Scandinavians also
developed a reputation for their
groundbreaking designs in plastic:
Eero Aarnio and Verner Panton.

Many Nordic industrial designers also worked in plastic,
not least Sigvard Bernadotte, a Swedish royal prince
and multi-talented designer who also worked in silver,
ceramics, glass, graphics and textiles. Bernadotte was
one of the founders of the Swedish Industrial Designers
Society and was also for many years president of ICSID,
the International Council of Societies of Industrial Design.
His plastic nesting Margrethe mixing bowls, designed for
the Danish company Rosti in 1950, are still in production
more than half a century later. (In fact the bowls were
dreamed up by Bernadotte's young assistant Jacob
Jensen, who was later to make Bang & Olufsen famous
with his sleek hi-fi designs.)

Another Bernadotte success story was the sturdy yet
sleek plastic Röda Clara wall-mounted tin opener, which
has been a standard piece of equipment in every Swedish
kitchen for the past half century. Bernadotte's influence
on Swedish design has been profound – even the exact
shade of blue on the carriages of the Stockholm Metro
was only chosen after consultation with Bernadotte.

The Finnish designer Eero Aarnio opened his interior
and industrial design studio in Helsinki in 1962. In 1963,
he designed the futuristic Ball chair (also known as the
Thunderball or Globe) made from moulded polyester-
reinforced fibreglass. Its material and form – a hollow
sphere on a stand with a cushioned interior – made it
a complete novelty for the furniture industry of the time,

above The Vitra Design
Museum has produced a
miniature of Eero Aarnio's
classic Ball chair, which the
designer proudly displays
in his home. Sitting inside
the chair blocks out all
surrounding sounds.

right The Margrethe mixing
bowl by the Danish company
Rosti was created by Jacob
Jensen in 1950 while he was
working for the designers
Sigvard Bernadotte and
Acton Bjørn. It has been in
production ever since. To
celebrate its 50th anniversary,
Rosti commissioned a bowl
in silver as a gift for Queen
Margrethe of Denmark.

left The Panthella floor lamp is produced by Louis Poulsen. It was originally introduced in a variety of different colours but the current production is only in white, lending it a timeless, classic air.

above Nanna Ditzel created several pieces for the Danish company Domus Danica in the late 1960s, including this curvaceous chair, which was produced in several different colours and versions.

even though fibreglass was already used in boat construction. The easy-to-work material enabled Aarnio to create furniture in unusual forms without the usual restrictions. With the creation of his bold, colourful Pastil, Bubble and Tomato chairs, Aarnio received international acclaim as furniture designer to the pop generation. The chairs can be used both indoors and out, and they float on water. They have been featured in numerous films over the last fifty years. Aarnio is still active as a designer, and his most famous work is now back in production again.

The well-known futuristic designs of the Danish designer Verner Panton range from the stacking moulded-plastic Panton chair – the very first example of a single-form moulded fibreglass chair (now made in polyurethane) – to the elegant acrylic Panthella lamps he created for Louis

Poulsen, to inflatable furniture and even attempts to create plastic houses. Although Panton will always be mainly associated with his innovative space-age designs of the 1960s, in reality his career spanned five productive decades. As trends in interiors shift away from sparse and minimal white interiors, the colour, energy and joie de vivre of Panton's designs have won them a new popularity.

The well-known futuristic designs in plastic of Danish designer Verner Panton range from the stacking moulded-plastic Panton chair – the first example of a single-form moulded chair – to acrylic Panthella lamps.

this page The Panton chair of 1960 signalled the beginning of the era of plastic furniture, but the concept of a chair crafted from a single piece of material had occupied several Danish designers throughout the 1950s.

LIGHT

The Nordic summer nights are warm and light, while the winter months are long and dark with only a few hours of weak sun every day. As a result, maximizing quality of light has been a preoccupation of many Scandinavian architects and designers.

opposite and below left
Poul Henningsen's model PH 5 from 1958 is just one in a long series of PH lamps, which began back in 1926. It has become the most popular model and is said to hang in half of all Danish homes.

right Because Scandinavia lies in the north of the northern hemisphere, and the sun hits the ground at an angle rather than from above, the light is diffused and weak. As a result, maximizing light is a priority in Scandinavian architecture. This room has two glass walls and enjoys the luxury of natural daylight throughout the day.

The Danish architect, designer and writer Poul Henningsen is unique in terms of the sheer volume of his lighting designs. Born in 1894, he designed his first PH light in the 1920s in cooperation with the company Louis Poulsen, and continued to work right up until his death in 1967. Henningsen was a political radical and his cooperation with Louis Poulsen was only possible due to the equally radical outlook of its managing director Sophus Kaastrup-Olsen. Both men saw it as their mission to bring electrical power and good-quality lighting to the masses – most working-class homes at the time had no electrical supply at all, or only a naked light bulb.

By the 1930s, the PH lamps were bestsellers, and many models are still in production today. The principle is simple: a carefully constructed shade screens the glare of the bulb while distributing light evenly around the room. The PH lamps appear in many Danish homes and public buildings, as well as in the work of Danish architects around the world, including the Sydney Opera House.

Most designs are discreet and classical, but Le Klint's collaboration with designer Poul Christiansen in the 1970s resulted in some playful, pop-art styles.

The only other lamps that have managed to compete with PH lamps in Danish homes are those produced by Le Klint, a small but successful family company. Founded in 1943 by Tage Klint, brother of the famous Danish furniture designer Kaare Klint, the company has worked with dozens of designers over the years to produce shades fashioned from pleated and hand-folded paper. Most of the designs are discreet and classical in feel, but Le Klint's collaboration with the designer Poul Christiansen in the 1970s resulted in some playful, pop-art styles that have recently enjoyed a new lease of life.

Arne Jacobsen was a close friend of Poul Henningsen's (they escaped the German occupation of Denmark together by crossing to Sweden in a rowing boat with their wives) and he was undoubtedly influenced by Henningsen's research into lighting distribution, especially as most of Jacobsen's lights were also produced by Louis Poulsen. Although Jacobsen is better known as a furniture designer and architect nowadays, he also produced a large number of lighting designs that were intended for several specific architectural projects.

this page The Stelling mouth-blown glass pendant is an early Arne Jacobsen design, manufactured by Louis Poulsen for the Stelling house in Copenhagen in 1937. The lamp was briefly reproduced during 2002 as part of the Arne Jacobsen centenary celebration and is already a collector's item.

this page and opposite left
The AJ table and floor lamps were designed by Arne Jacobsen and made by Louis Poulsen for the SAS Royal Hotel, Copenhagen. The circular foot was designed to hold an ashtray. The thin stem was a difficult achievement at a time when electrical wiring was thicker than it is today.

right Arne Jacobsen designed St Catherine's College in Oxford, England, in the early 1960s. The Oxford lamp was designed for the students' reading desks and was mounted directly into the wooden tables without a foot. Louis Poulsen later made a limited production of the lamp with a circular foot.

Although Arne Jacobsen is better known as a furniture designer and architect, he also designed a large number of lights for specific projects.

The Stelling glass pendant of 1937 was briefly reissued in 2002, but otherwise only a few of Jacobsen's lights are still in production, such as the AJ lamp series created for the SAS Royal Hotel in Copenhagen and the Munkegard ceiling lamp for the Munkegard school. Some Jacobsen lamps have been reissued by Spanish company Santa & Cole, including the circular metallic Aarhus lamp, which he designed for Aarhus city hall in the 1930s.

Finnish designers expended great effort on their lighting designs. Alvar Aalto was also a friend of Henningsen's and adapted the idea of a multi-shade system to suit his own architectural style. Like Jacobsen, he created most of his lighting designs for specific architectural projects, and many are still in production by Aalto's company, Artek, which he co-founded in 1935. Tapio Wirkkala also

opposite The PH Snowball was designed by Poul Henningsen for Louis Poulsen in 1958.

left When Verner Panton first designed the Panthella lamps for Louis Poulsen, he used the same size shade for the table and floor lamps, but soon realized that the proportions did not work. Later table lamps, like this one, have smaller shades.

right The Moon lamp was designed by Verner Panton for Louis Poulsen in the 1960s. The overlapping shade is reminiscent of Poul Henningsen's designs for the Copenhagen Tivoli during the war, which required that no light was visible from the air.

left Danish designer Finn Juhl experimented with product design outside furniture, but only a handful of pieces made it into production. This table lamp from 1963 was produced by the Danish company Lyfa. The bottom part of the shade can be tilted to adjust the direction of the light.

opposite The Norwegian company Luxo made many different versions of the L-1 desk lamp, designed by the company's founder Jac Jacobsen. The basic principle of two arms and a spring system was a German invention but Jacobsen added some Scandinavian design talent and successful marketing.

For a while during the 1940s and 1950s, the L-1 dominated the world market in desk lamps, and its success has helped Luxo to become a world leader in lighting designed especially for the workplace.

worked on lighting designs, as did the Le Corbusier-trained designer Ilmari Tapiovaara, but the most prolific Finnish lighting designer was Lisa Johansson-Pape. Born in 1907, she originally trained and worked as a furniture designer. In 1930 she visited the Stockholm Exhibition, which was a turning point in her life. From the 1940s she worked for the Orno lighting factory and designed an endless series of glass, textile, metal and plastic lamps, both for domestic and public use. Johansson-Pape was particularly skilled at tastefully and tactfully installing contemporary lighting in historical buildings, a talent which won her the job of lighting consultant to the great mosque in Mecca during the 1970s. Her expertise in lighting took her on lecture tours and exhibitions around the world, and there are many Finnish homes that still use Johansson-Pape lights manufactured by Orno.

Another great Orno lighting designer was Yki Nummi, the son of a Finnish missionary born in China in 1925. Between 1950 and 1958, for Orno, he designed lamps for hospitals, sanatoriums, churches and offices. Between 1951 and 1965, Nummi developed a series of transparent acrylic lamps: the Modern Art table lamp from 1956 was exhibited at MoMA, while his futuristic Sky Flyer from 1960 is now back in production again.

Luxo is the largest lighting company in Norway, built on the success of its founder, Jac Jacobsen (no relation to Arne Jacobsen) and his L-1 desk lamp, designed in 1937. The L-1 was principally an adaptation of earlier Bauhaus designs, but Jacobsen managed to improve both the function and aesthetics of the light. The concept of two jointed arms controlled by springs and with a heavy base or clamp to hold the lamp in place has now become a standard design for almost all desk lamps. For a while during the 1940s and 1950s, the Luxo L-1 dominated the world market in desk lamps, and its success has helped Luxo to become a world leader in lighting designed especially for the workplace.

The BASQUE HISTORY of the WORLD
A LIFE OF PICASSO
JOHN RICHARDSON
THE IVY The Restaurant and its Recipes
AA GILL
LA VIE ET L'OEUVRE DE MODIGLIANI
TÀPIES

LIVING

Mikael Andersen

Built like a strictly symmetrical wooden box, this unique building is situated close to the sea on Nordsjælland, north of Copenhagen in Denmark.

When gallery owner Mikael Andersen wanted to create a haven of tranquillity where his artist friends could work without distraction, he called on one of the world's most celebrated architects, the legendary Henning Larsen. It is unusual for such a well-known and long-established architect to undertake a small-scale domestic project, but it is obvious that this project was something of a labour of love for Larsen. His building stands in a grove of larch trees and is surrounded by over 200 newly planted birches.

Henning Larsen worked for two of the greatest names in Danish 20th-century architecture – Arne Jacobsen and Jørn Utzon – before he set up his own studio in 1959. Today, Henning Larsen Architects employs more than 100 people. His most famous building is the Saudi Arabian Foreign Ministry in Riyadh, a monumental, fortress-like structure that marries together Danish and Islamic styles. Recent projects include the Danish Design Centre and the new Opera House in Copenhagen.

The house he designed for Andersen is a single space of approximately 100 square metres/1000 square feet. A central kitchen and toilet block divides the space into two halves: an artists' studio and a living area. If necessary, sliding doors can further subdivide the interior into four rooms. Large terraces run along two sides of the house.

left The south-facing window is a single sheet of glass that allows natural light to flood into the interior. The sea is about 70 metres/230 feet away, on the other side of the fringe of wild grass that has been planted around the house. The sofa and desk are from Cappellini and the floor lamp is an Arne Jacobsen design for Louis Poulsen.

this page At the centre of the space is a small, self-contained kitchen and toilet block with a fireplace on each side. The walls and ceiling are covered with laminated birch.

opposite above left Along the side of the building, five sections of the wall can be opened and closed individually to control the flow of light.

opposite above right Four sliding doors can divide the house into four sections. The aluminium chairs are for use both on the terrace outside and inside the house.

opposite below right The kitchen is small but well planned. The stainless-steel handles on the cupboards were designed by Arne Jacobsen in the late 1960s for the National Bank in Copenhagen.

opposite below left The concept of the house is to function as a retreat for Danish and international artists. With its quiet surroundings and excellent natural lighting, the house allows the guests to focus entirely on their work.

Mikael Andersen wanted to create a haven of tranquillity where his artist friends could work without distraction.

Larsen is known for his unique way of working with light by bringing daylight into buildings. In the northern hemisphere, the sun comes in at an angle and creates a soft, translucent light, so people strive to let in as much daylight as possible. In the house Larsen has created for Mikael Andersen, this aim is evident. The largest window in the house faces south and is 15 square metres/160 square feet in size. On the long side of the building, five sections of the wood-clad wall can be raised to let the daylight flood in. When closed, the building resembles a boat with all the hatches tightly battened down for a storm.

left Along the outside of the house, five hatches can be opened to allow in varying amounts of natural daylight.

below left The house is clad in larch wood and has a flat roof that is angled just enough to allow rainwater to drain off.

this page Andersen's neighbours have affectionately named the house the 'cigar box'. The surrounding land has been planted with 200 birch trees and wild grass.

left As in many Danish houses, the stove is a freestanding feature.

right On top of the bookshelves stand glass prototypes by Grethe Meyer. The sofa, Model 2213, was designed by Børge Mogensen in 1962 for his own home, and is now produced by Fredericia Furniture. It is Mogensen's best-selling sofa and is a standard in Danish embassies around the world. The coffee table is another Mogensen classic, also dating from 1962.

Grethe Meyer

The home of Grethe Meyer, Denmark's foremost ceramic designer, showcases her own designs as well as furniture designed by her close friend, designer Børge Mogensen.

Grethe Meyer's home was designed in the 1960s by a group of Danish architects. It is entirely characteristic of its time, with simple white brickwork and an open floor plan. Whitewashed floorboards provide a restrained backdrop for the furniture. Many pieces are by celebrated Danish designer Børge Mogensen (see pages 94–99). Meyer and Mogensen were close friends and collaborated on several furniture projects.

The two designers shared many beliefs and ideals. Like Mogensen's, Grethe Meyer's work espouses practicality, simplicity and harmony. Their joint work for the Danish Consumer Co-operative in the 1950s attempted to provide inexpensive yet good-quality furniture that could be sold as standardized modules. Their best-known collaboration is the Boligens Byggeskabe wall unit, which dates from 1952 and is now a modern classic.

this page and left The large shelving unit is filled with a beautiful collection of old and new ceramics, all designed by Grethe Meyer. The large, rounded bowls are part of her Blå Kant (Blue Line) collection. Suspended above the table is the PH 5 pendant lamp by Poul Henningsen; one is said to hang in every second Danish home. The Shaker table and chairs are by Børge Mogensen for the Danish Consumer Co-operative in 1944.

Meyer's home is practical, unpretentious and comfortable. The countless pieces of china and glass – all her own designs – are not precious objects to be handled with care. Instead, they are used just as Meyer intended them to be – every single day.

Grethe Meyer (1918–2008) trained as an architect, but from the 1960s she became best-known for her ceramics, mainly produced for Royal Copenhagen. At a time when the decorative style of the 1950s began to fall from favour, Meyer's simple, rustic designs were in tune with public taste. Today, her style is still in demand. Her faience tableware series Blå Kant (Blue Line) of 1965 provided Royal Copenhagen with a bestseller that remained in production until 2011 (under the name '4 All Seasons'). Another popular Meyer design is her Copenhagen cutlery, designed for Georg Jensen in 1991.

Grethe Meyer's own home reflected her design ethos in every way. It was practical, unpretentious and very comfortable. The countless pieces of china and glass out on display – all her own designs – were not treated as precious objects to be handled with care. Instead, they were used just as Meyer intended them to be – every single day.

above left The Øresund kitchen system, designed by Børge Mogensen and Grethe Meyer, displays a collection of Meyer's own ceramics. When the Blå Kant (Blue Line) series was introduced in 1965, the range came in a single colour, but later the series was renamed '4 All Seasons' and produced in a multitude of different shades, as can be seen on the two top shelves.

above right The brass pendant lamp is another of Meyer's own designs. It hangs in front of stacks of teacups from the Blå Kant series.

above Blå Kant (Blue Line) bowls and Ocean vases by Grethe Meyer are ranged along the top shelf. The side table is by Børge Mogensen.

right The 1952 Boligens Byggeskabe wall unit was designed by Grethe Meyer and Børge Mogensen. It became a bestseller and broke new ground in modular storage systems. The geometric Side by Side dishes in the foreground were made by Grethe Meyer for Royal Copenhagen in 1996 but never put into mass production.

this page The large Kuutti Lavonen painting is entitled 'Regina Celi'. Stacked on the floor are two large cushions from the Woodnotes collection.

opposite The dining table is by Antonio Citterio for B&B Italia, while the wood-fibre rugs from the Woodnotes collection were designed by Ritva Puotila.

Mikko Puotila

With a new floor plan, an ordinary flat in Espoo, Finland, has been transformed into an open-plan space that offers both flexible and comfortable family living.

Mikko Puotila runs Woodnotes, a company he set up with his mother, Finnish textile designer Ritva Puotila. Her large-scale textile artworks can be seen in many institutions and corporate headquarters both in Finland and abroad. Ritva Puotila first began experimenting with wood fibre as a textile material in the 1960s, and in the late 1980s she and Mikko Puotila took the bold decision to establish a company producing items made from the material.

When Ritva and Mikko Puotila set up Woodnotes, wood fibre was an unfashionable, utilitarian material, associated with hard times. Wood fibre had been used in Finland to replace imported cotton during the war and was also used to insulate underground telephone cables. The Puotilas managed to purchase the last factory in

Finland specializing in wood-fibre insulated cables, and converted the 30-year-old machinery to make wood-fibre rugs. Woodnotes is now a successful company that exports the majority of its products. It produces blinds, rugs, furniture, placemats, table runners and bags, all crafted from humble wood fibre.

When Mikko Puotila, together with his girlfriend and baby son, moved into an apartment in Espoo, in the south of Finland, they called on interior architect Ulla Koskinen for advice. Although the building, which dated from 1981, was designed by the well-known architects Gullichsen-Kairamo-Vormala, the floor plan of their new apartment

Mikko Puotila has furnished his home with Scandinavian design classics and a selection of pieces from Woodnotes.

opposite With simple crockery and a Woodnotes runner, the table setting has an oriental flavour. The tall console table offers display space, but also keeps treasures out of the reach of small fingers. The bookshelves were custom built.

above left Sliding doors lead to the master bedroom, which was created by removing a wall between two smaller rooms. The sofa is by B&B Italia.

above right The kitchen has a sea view but the main worksurface overlooks the living room. Black Series 7 chairs and an Eero Saarinen Tulip table are used for informal meals.

needed a rethink. The flat consisted of several small rooms and a narrow kitchen. Mikko Puotila wanted to transform it into an open space generously lit with natural daylight and with uninterrupted views of the nearby sea.

Ulla Koskinen came up with the idea of relocating the kitchen in a bedroom with an en-suite bathroom, which meant that the existing plumbing could be utilized. The wall between two small bedrooms was removed to create one large master bedroom suite. All the internal doors were replaced or simply removed, and some of the doorways were widened, to increase the sense of space. Finally, an oiled oak floor was laid, and Puotila's son now has plenty of uninterrupted floor space to play on.

All the internal doors were replaced or removed, and some of the doorways were widened, to increase the feeling of space. Finally, skirting boards were removed before an oiled oak floor was laid.

Mikko Puotila has furnished his home with many Scandinavian design classics, including Arne Jacobsen's Series 7 chairs and Vola taps and a Saarinen table, teamed with modern Italian designs and, of course, a selection of pieces from Woodnotes, including floor cushions, rugs and seating cubes. The only Woodnotes products used sparingly are their blinds – after all, the views of the Baltic Sea outside are just too good to hide.

left Like so many Finnish homes, this one has its own sauna. More than just a hot room for cleansing the body, the sauna is used for relaxation and social gatherings, with cold drinks close to hand.

opposite A room with a view – the bathroom looks out over the Baltic Sea. The tub is clad in wenge wood and the sleek Vola tap/faucet is by Arne Jacobsen. The floor and walls are clad in marble tiles and a sandblasted glass screen acts as a room divider.

Finn Juhl and Hanne Wilhelm Hansen

Legendary Danish architect and designer Finn Juhl designed his home in the 1940s, sharing it with Hanne Wilhelm Hansen from 1960. The house is an enduring testament to their shared design philosophy.

The house is filled with many of Juhl's most famous pieces, set against whitewashed wooden floors and plain white walls. The simplicity of the backdrop provides a dramatic contrast with his classic designs, such as the Chieftain chair. Ceramics, wooden bowls and glass objects are dotted around the house, most of which were also designed by Juhl. The bookshelves and cupboards were custom made and most of the lighting is by Juhl. Even the rugs are by Finn Juhl. While Juhl designed the building and most of the objects inside it, Hansen chose much of the artwork.

Born in Copenhagen in 1912, Juhl studied architecture at the Royal Academy of Fine Arts before starting to work for the architect Wilhelm Lauritzen. Between 1935 and 1945, Juhl assisted Lauritzen with his designs for Copenhagen Airport and the Danish Broadcasting Corporation building, two of the most important building projects in Denmark at that time.

After the war, in 1945, Juhl left Lauritzen's practice to start his own and became an increasingly important name in Scandinavian design. He was responsible for the interiors

opposite Juhl's 45 Chairs (in front of the table) were produced by Niels Vodder in 1945. The armchairs on either side were designed in 1944 and only 12 copies were ever made. The wooden bowl was designed by Juhl in 1951 and produced by master turner Magne Monsen.

this page The home office is fitted with custom-made bookshelves. Above the desk hangs a lighting pendant designed by Wilhelm Lauritzen for the Danish Broadcasting Corporation building.

above The Chieftain chair of 1949 is perhaps the best-known of all Juhl's designs. Its distinctive form was directly influenced by African shields.

right Above the Poet sofa of 1941 hangs a portrait of Hanne Wilhelm Hansen aged 17, painted by Vilhelm Lundstrøm, a good friend of Juhl's whose work he often used in his interiors. On the floor lies Juhl's Domino rug.

of the Georg Jensen showrooms in New York, Toronto and London, as well as the interiors of over thirty Scandinavian Airlines System (SAS) ticket offices round the world. He also designed the interior of the Danish ambassador's residence in Washington, D. C. and the Trusteeship Council Chamber in the United Nations headquarters in New York.

At the same time, Juhl was pouring out designs for furniture, lighting and other pieces, many of which were used in his interiors. His style was radically different to that of other furniture designers of the time and at the start of his career was considered positively controversial.

far left This sofa was first shown at the Cabinetmaker's Guild in Copenhagen in 1948. It is made from maple and Cuban mahogany with cowhide. The matching armchair was later produced by Baker Furniture in the USA. By the window on the left stands a small table designed by Nanna Ditzel.

left This coloured cabinet is part of a storage system designed by Juhl in 1974. Only a few were ever made. This was one of Juhl's last designs, but it still looks distinctly modern today.

African arts and craft, together with historical Japanese, Chinese and Egyptian furniture, were all important influences.

African arts and craft, together with historical Japanese, Chinese and Egyptian furniture, were all important influences.

Beech is the wood most commonly used for Danish furniture because it is easy to work with and readily available, thus inexpensive. Juhl chose to experiment with exotic woods such as maple, cherry, cedar, palisander, walnut and even teak, which was normally only used for outdoor furniture. For over twenty years Juhl collaborated with Danish master cabinetmaker Niels Vodder. Together, they developed new methods of joining and bending wood and combining it with leather, cane and upholstery. The results were always beautiful, but not always suitable for mass production. Today, Finn Juhl designs produced by Niels Vodder are among the most sought-after of all Danish mid-century furniture designs. Two other Danish companies – France & Son and Bovirke – also produced Juhl's furniture. From 1950, Finn Juhl furniture was produced in the USA by Baker Furniture, and Juhl even designed the company's showroom in Grand Rapids.

Finn Juhl died in 1989 and Hanne Hansen in 2009, but his reputation is still growing. Finn Juhl furniture is once again being made in Denmark, while their home remains a testament to the talent and energy of an exceptional designer and an exceptional couple.

left Sanaksenaho's home blends into its surroundings like a birdwatcher's hide.

above Finnish pines surround the Finnish-pine façade. The timber was heat-treated to ensure it was perfectly dry and provides good insulation against bad weather.

opposite above right The flat roof is tilted just enough to prevent snow from building up during the winter. The curved front makes reference to Aalto's Finlandia Hall, but on a domestic scale.

Matti Sanaksenaho

The forest home of architect Matti Sanaksenaho is an example of the very best of modern Finnish architecture. Designed to bring the forest outside into the interior, the house is totally integrated into the surrounding landscape.

Even though the home of architect Matti Sanaksenaho is only a modest 150 square metres/1600 square feet in size, there is absolutely nothing modest about Sanaksenaho's professional achievements. He was the man behind the highly acclaimed wood-clad Finnish pavilion at the World Exhibition in Seville in 1992 and he was also responsible for creating the flagship store on the Esplanade in Helsinki for Designor, the company that owned Iittala, maker of the Alvar Aalto vases. Sanaksenaho also designed the Designor shop in Stockholm. Anyone who has seen these two stores would immediately recognize their similarities with Sanaksenaho's own home, but this is not surprising, as Designor's brief was to make the stores look as though someone lived there.

Sanaksenaho's home is located in Espoo, not far from Helsinki but far enough away to enjoy proper forest surroundings and a view over nearby lakes. Matti Sanaksenaho lives in the house with his family and has a small studio upstairs. The concept was not to build a grand mansion, but to create a family home that was completely integrated with the surrounding landscape. A terrace and a balcony add to the sense of space, while the large windows and expanses of glass bring the landscape inside. On warm days, meals and social gatherings are enjoyed outside.

The house was completed in 2002 and took about a year to build. The exterior is completely clad with Finnish pine, which was first heat-treated to ensure that it was completely dry and proof against any later warping or shrinkage. Pine is a good insulator that provides suitable protection against changing weather conditions, be they extreme heat or cold. Inside the house the floor, parts of the ceiling and the gallery are crafted from birch, the classic Finnish wood, which also appears in the form of the birch furniture used throughout Sanaksenaho's home. The house has triple glazing throughout – a standard Finnish domestic feature, along with having a sauna in the basement (another feature of this house). A heating system has been built into the ceiling of the 7m/20ft-high living room to project warmth downwards, and there are radiators built into the floor just below the large windows. This very effective and efficient heating system has been teamed with a large open fireplace for visual warmth and interest.

this page The ceiling and gallery are clad with birch wood, the wood Alvar Aalto favoured for his furniture. In front of the bar stand two model K 65 kitchen stools designed by Aalto for Artek in 1933–35. The open-plan kitchen leads straight into the living area. Behind the curtain is a double door opening onto a large terrace, allowing summer meals to be enjoyed alfresco.

The curved façade of Sanaksenaho's house is certainly reminiscent of Finlandia Hall, Alvar Aalto's last large-scale building project in Helsinki.

Sanaksenaho's home makes obvious references to the work of Alvar Aalto, but then Aalto himself was greatly influenced by the Finnish landscape, so it is not surprising that anyone building a house in a Finnish forest would somehow refer to Aalto's natural, organic style.

The broad, curved façade of Sanaksenaho's house is certainly reminiscent of Finlandia Hall, a concert hall that was Aalto's last large-scale building project in Helsinki.

Sanaksenaho's house is very representative of modern Finnish architecture. It expresses a desire to bring the landscape indoors and to be close to nature, to enjoy plenty of natural daylight yet be able to gather round a warm fire on dark, cold winter nights. These needs and yearnings are deeply rooted in the Finnish psyche and hold the key to the beauty and integrity of Finnish architecture and design.

this page The total ceiling height of the living room is an impressive seven metres. In front of the birch-clad gallery hangs a PH 5 light by Poul Henningsen.

opposite Upstairs is a work area with a view of the forest. The chair is a Model 68 by Alvar Aalto, designed in 1933–35 and upholstered with a zebra-patterned fabric also designed by Aalto.

Børge and Alice Mogensen

Børge Mogensen's work could never be described as lighthearted or flirtatious, but his own home shows that his furniture can be both elegant and casual at the same time. It is very Danish but also very international, drawing on influences from Spain, China and America.

opposite By the fireplace sits a 1962 Conference easy chair in teak. Behind is a Boligens Byggeskabe wall unit from 1952, designed by Børge Mogensen and Grethe Meyer.

below A dining chair designed in 1951 sits in front of the oak Shaker table.

Børge and Alice Mogensen's home was built in 1958 and was designed by Børge Mogensen himself. He created his home in very much the same way as he created his famous furniture, starting by first considering its function and construction. The house has a passing resemblance to a finca – a traditional Spanish farmhouse. There is also a parallel between the appearance of the furniture and the house it sits in: nothing is hidden, nothing is concealed. The oak floor boards were whitewashed and left to age naturally, as was the beech timber ceiling. The brick walls have been whitewashed to stop the bricks from dusting, but the brickwork is still clearly visible. Parts of the house have tiled floors, but few rugs are laid to soften the lines. Most windows are free of blinds or curtains.

Mogensen's design ethos was practical yet political. His thinking was similar to that of the lighting designer Poul Henningsen, who wanted to create goods that would benefit the masses. In contrast to designers like Finn Juhl, who saw each chair as a piece of art, the furniture Mogensen designed was always intended for mass production, albeit a very Danish type of high-quality mass production. One of Mogensen's closest friends was designer Hans Wegner, and their furniture shares a desire to honestly reveal every last join and plug of the construction.

Børge Mogensen was just one of many famous Danish designers who studied under Kaare Klint at the furniture faculty at the Royal Academy of Fine Arts.

this page Børge Mogensen designed this sofa, Model 2213, for his own home. It went on to become his best-selling sofa and can be seen in Danish embassies around the world. The coffee table is another Mogensen classic, dating from 1962. In front sit two Spanish chairs in oak with leather seats, designed in 1959. The chair is Mogensen's Danish adaptation of a traditional Spanish design. They work particularly well in his house, which makes strong references to Mediterranean architecture.

above A dividing wall that stops just short of the slanting ceiling divides the kitchen from the dining area. The Shaker table and chairs were designed by Børge Mogensen in 1944 for the Danish Consumer Co-operative, where Mogensen was head of furniture design between 1942 and 1950. The chair is considered a landmark in Danish furniture design.

above right The sharply sloping ceilings of the house create dramatic angles and unexpected perspectives.

Klint's teachings included proportional studies to assess the interaction between humans and furniture, and the historical development of furniture. It is thanks to Kaare Klint that a generation of Danish designers was inspired and influenced by Chinese, Spanish, Egyptian, English and American furniture designs. After completing his studies in 1941, Mogensen worked as an assistant to Klint before he took on the position of head of furniture design at the Danish Consumer Co-operative. His work at the Co-op included furniture lines for young children sold under names like 'Peter's Room' and 'Hansen's Attic'. He is also credited with ending the Danish weakness for fake mahogany by introducing beech and oak.

In 1952 Mogensen, in collaboration with Grethe Meyer, created a modular shelving and storage system called Boligens Byggeskabe. Mogensen thoroughly researched standard measures for objects such as crockery and shoes, and how many items of each the average person owned. With this information, he established the optimum size of drawers and shelves and published manuals on storage systems. Between 1955 and 1967, Mogensen developed the Øresund series, which took on the gargantuan task of resolving every storage problem in a home. It is still produced by Karl Andersson & Söner in Sweden.

By the end of the 1950s, Mogensen's designs were slowly edging towards a purer form of functionalism that

right The Hunting chair was designed in 1950 for the annual Danish Cabinetmakers' Guild Exhibition.

below Sofa Model 1789 was designed by Mogensen in 1945 and is made by Fritz Hansen. Like most upholstered Mogensen furniture, it is covered with fabric designed by Lis Ahlmann.

opposite Poul Henningsen's PH 5 lamp is a common feature in Danish homes.

Parts of the house have tiled floors, but few rugs are laid to soften the lines. Windows are free of blinds or curtains.

was quite unusual at the time. His furniture designs became increasingly pared-down, severe and square, and were less inspired by historical references. However, during the 1960s and 1970s, Mogensen's more austere style became a standard for Danish design. Without having to compromise on his design ethos, Mogensen's furniture grew increasingly popular with upper middle-class Danes and with official and corporate Denmark, and has remained so to this day. Børge and Alice Mogensen's home serves as a reminder of the many different facets of his work and of his journey from Danish Modern to simply modern.

left A small wooden Dala horse sits on the coffee table, a symbol of traditional Swedish crafts. The O rug is by Matz Borgström for Asplund.

above Wedding stools by Thomas Sandell for Asplund are a modern take on traditional farmhouse furniture. On top are two mugs by Alfredo Häberli for Rörstrand.

Michael Asplund

The Stockholm home of furniture manufacturer and retailer Michael Asplund is filled with pieces that reveal the radical shift in Swedish design over the last decade; distinctly Swedish but with an injection of Italian style.

Many of the objects in Asplund's home enjoy design-classic status due to the efforts of Michael and his brother Thomas. Through their joint company, simply called Asplund, which they founded in the late 1980s, the Asplunds manufacture and retail modern design. The emphasis is on Sweden and Italy, but they work with international designers from all over the world. As a consequence of his work, almost all the objects in his home are designed by people Michael Asplund knows personally, and are either from the Asplund collection or are sourced from Italy for the Asplund store in central Stockholm.

Rugs and textiles are an important part of the Asplund collection, and important international designers such as Jasper Morrison, Tom Dixon and Marc Newson have contributed designs. The well-known Swedish architect and designer Thomas Sandell produces designs for Asplund and there are several of his pieces in Asplund's apartment.

this page The Italian sofa and table are flanked by Alvar Aalto stools and a Crux rug by Pia Wallén for Asplund. Like many Stockholm apartments dating from the first half of the last century, this one has a parquet floor, which has been restored to its original beauty.

opposite Chairs by Thomas Sandell for Asplund surround the dining table. The shelves behind display glass designs by Ann Wåhlström, Gunnel Sahlin, Ingegerd Råman and Tom Dixon. The pendant lamp is by Jonas Bohlin.

this page These Slowfox vases by Ingegerd Råman for Orrefors are decorated with a thin, hand-held sand-blasting pen, making every vase slightly different to the next.

The Snow series of cabinets by Sandell and fellow Swedish designer Jonas Bohlin is one of the most successful Asplund products, and they appear throughout the apartment in the form of bookshelves, bedside tables and storage units. The cut-out design of their handles is reminiscent of a smiling mouth and bring a spontaneity and humour to the interior.

The Asplund brothers have been particularly active in the revival of Swedish glass design, staging exhibitions and commissioning special pieces for their store, and the apartment contains a selection of the glass Asplund has promoted, including vases by Gunnel Sahlin and Ann Wåhlström for Kosta Boda and by Ingegerd Råman for Orrefors, the two most prominent Swedish glassworks.

While white is the dominant colour in the apartment, textiles and wood bring warmth and life to the interior.

There is a serenity and calm in the interior that makes it easy on the eye and far removed from stark minimalism. Most of the furniture and accessories are either from Asplund's own collection or are sourced from Italy for his Asplund store.

Another Swedish designer with close links to Asplund is Pia Wallén, and her rugs, throws, slippers and cushions can be found throughout Michael Asplund's home.

There is a serenity and calm to the interior that makes it easy on the eye, yet the decor is far removed from stark minimalism. While white is the dominant colour, textiles and wood bring warmth and life to the interior. The parquet floor is original, as is the open fireplace, which is regularly used during the winter months. Asplund has been a keen follower of the Swedish and international modern art scene for many years, and his home is decorated with a selection of framed artworks and photography.

The housing stock in central Stockholm tends to be quite consistent in style, as most housing was either built during the economic boom of 1890-1910 or between 1935 and 1955, when housing associations first came into existence. Housing development was geographically limited due to the city's location on a group of islands, with the more recently built suburbs set apart from the city centre. Functionalist houses from the 1930s on are increasingly popular, because they were well built and planned, and have period details that younger generations now appreciate. Door handles are often made in wood, windows are large, and communal staircases tend to be crafted from marble or local stone. Balconies are standard in both small and larger apartments. Asplund has used the original period features of his home to great advantage, and the contemporary furnishings underline the building's heritage.

Outside, a large balcony overlooks Södermalm, one of the large islands that make up central Stockholm. Traditionally a working-class district, Södermalm is now very popular, due to its pleasant and convivial mix of small shops, bars and restaurants, which bring people into the neighbourhood. Nearby is Mariatorget, a tree-lined square with fountains that is a regular venue for improvised boule tournaments during the summer months.

opposite A row of cabinets designed by Jonas Bohlin and Thomas Sandell for the Asplund furniture collection, offer plenty of practical storage space, while the distinct cut-out 'handles' bring a smile to the room.

this page In the main bedroom, the bed is covered with a Cross throw by Pia Wallén. Hand-woven in southern Sweden from wool collected from local animals, these throws have a weight and density that machine-made throws cannot match, and are something of an icon of modern Swedish design.

Poul and Hanne Kjærholm

Just north of Copenhagen, along the coastline that overlooks Sweden and the Øresund strait, is a well-kept neighbourhood dotted with a string of villas built by some of the greatest names in Danish architecture.

Villa Kjærholm might not be the largest but it is certainly one of the best-planned buildings in the area. It is also the perfect backdrop for the furniture Poul Kjærholm designed during his 30-year career. The house itself was designed in 1962 by his wife, Hanne Kjærholm, an architect and professor at the Art Academy. Poul Kjærholm died in 1980 and Hanne in 2009, but remarkably little has been changed since the house was built.

The most striking feature of the house is its close proximity to the water and its uninterrupted views of the ever-changing scenery. Inside, wooden ceiling beams

left The black PK 0 chair in moulded wood is one of the few Kjærholm designs that does not use steel. Never put into mass production, it is a sculpture as much as a chair. In front of the PK 31/2 leather sofa stands a PK 61 table with a glass top and steel legs. Kjærholm designed the wooden screen on the right especially for the house.

right The PK 24 chaise-longue in woven wicker sits on a delicate stainless-steel frame. The seat angle can be easily adjusted, while the tubular leather headrest cushion is held in place with a weight.

left The screen was designed especially for the house.

above A light fitting by architect Wilhelm Lauritzen.

right Around a PK 54 table sit several PK 9 chairs. Above the table hangs a PH Cascade lamp. Like many Danish designers, Kjærholm used Poul Henningsen's PH light fittings for Louis Poulsen.

Pieces like the PK 54 have a high level of engineering to them because Kjærholm avoided obvious design solutions without making the end result look contrived or overdesigned.

contrast with the whitewashed walls and the huge glass windows overlooking the water. The house is furnished with many of Kjærholm's own designs, which have developed a rich patina that proves how well modern design can age. The intransigent attitude of Kjærholm's designs remains impressive today: his furniture makes no compromises in terms of quality or function.

Kjærholm was taught both by the designer Hans Wegner and by Jørn Utzon – the architect responsible for Sydney Opera House – at the Art College in Copenhagen in the late 1940s. After leaving college he worked for Wegner and then for Utzon. In 1955 he embarked upon what was to be his most important collaboration, with the manufacturer Ejvind Kold Christensen. Together they developed some of the most striking and unusual furniture to come out of Scandinavia during this period. Despite his work with the great craftsman Hans Wegner and the prevailing trends of the time, Kjærholm's furniture is based around hard, unyielding materials such as steel, glass, marble and slate. Although they were designed during the 1950s and 1960s his pieces have a timeless integrity that means they still look fresh and modern today.

opposite A PK 11 chair from 1957 sits in front of the desk. To the left stands an Oregon pine sideboard by Mogens Koch.

left The PK 1 chair is unusual among Kjærholm's chairs in that it was manufacturered by PP Møbler rather than Ejvind Kold Christensen.

right An Alvar Aalto bar stool stands in the kitchen.

The house is furnished with many of Kjærholm's own designs, which have developed a rich patina that proves how well modern design can age.

Villa Kjærholm contains examples of the best of Kjærholm's designs. The PK 54 dining table consists of a large, round flint-rolled slab of marble set upon a satin-brushed stainless-steel frame. Six solid maple leaves slot in around the marble centre, increasing the size of the table to more than 2m/6ft in diameter. When not needed, the leaves can be stored away in a floor-standing rack, rather like a giant set of playing cards or a Japanese sculpture. Pieces like the PK 54 have a high level of engineering to them, because Kjærholm avoided obvious design solutions without making the end result look contrived or overdesigned.

Today, the manufacturer Fritz Hansen has taken over the production of Kjærholm's furniture designs, but his son, Thomas Kjærholm, still oversees production to ensure that nothing is altered. Not even the palette of leather colours Poul Kjærholm chose for his designs can be changed. It is easy to respect this faithfulness to Kjærholm's memory; his work was based on a precise attention to detail and it is a heritage worth upholding.

Christer Wallensteen

In a 1961 Sven Markelius building in central Stockholm, Christer Wallensteen has transformed a cramped and outdated office space into an airy home for himself and his two daughters. Modern classics and junk-shop finds are mixed with a selection of contemporary pieces.

Sven Markelius was one of the most innovative Swedish architects of the 20th century. He was one of the first to work with concrete back in the 1920s, and his buildings can be found all over Stockholm.

As City Architect during the 1950s and 1960s, Markelius was partly responsible for the complete destruction of some 160 buildings in the heart of Stockholm, some of them dating back to the 17th century. The bold new city grid destroyed the narrow and cramped old street plan, and replaced it with wide car-friendly thoroughfares lined with car parks and office blocks. This chapter in Stockholm's architectural history is something many inhabitants look back upon with great indignation, not least because most of the new buildings that replaced the old were not designed by Markelius and are of poor architectural quality. It could be argued that Markelius was a better architect than City Architect; his own buildings are held in much higher esteem than the city plan he implemented.

opposite The fireplace is so large that it houses the Bang & Olufsen television and the hi-fi system as well as a bookshelf, and also functions as a room divider. A Flexform sofa is positioned behind a coffee table by Hans Wegner. The original parquet flooring has been renovated and is a work of art in itself. To the left is the dining area, which leads to the open-plan kitchen.

right The colour scheme is kept strictly neutral, with furniture in grey and beige set against white walls. Modern and ultra-modern Danish design sits happily alongside each other in the sitting room.

The interior remains true to its functionalist heritage, retaining the original marble windowsills and beautiful parquet flooring.

One such Markelius building is the one in which Christer Wallensteen lives with his two daughters. When Wallensteen found the apartment, it had been used as an office for many years, despite the fact that the rest of the building is given over to residential use. Seven small rooms have since been converted into three large, spacious ones, together with an open-plan living room and kitchen. The interior remains true to its functionalist heritage, retaining the original marble windowsills and beautiful parquet flooring. Wallensteen also retained a dividing wall inset with rippled glass, very Sixties in style but entirely modern in spirit. His greatest triumph was to discover that the huge ventilation pipe that projected through his planned living space could be converted into an massive open fireplace. It is so large that it holds the TV, hi-fi system and built-in bookshelves, as well as functioning as a room divider.

Christer Wallensteen has furnished this space with neutral pieces in pale hues together with some modern classics, such as the Le Corbusier LC4 chaise-longue and Hans Wegner's CH 25 wicker easy chair. Other pieces include second-hand treasures such as a plastic string chair dating from the 1950s and a coffee table by

above The rippled glass internal window is part of the original interior by Sven Markelius, dating back to 1961. In front is a quirky and colourful second-hand chair dating from the 1950s and in the background is a Le Corbusier chaise-longue covered in pony skin.

opposite In the foreground stands a CH 25 chair by Hans Wegner, designed in 1951 for Carl Hansen & Søn in Denmark. When Christer Wallensteen renovated the Haga Terminal building, he used dozens of Wegner chairs. On the wall are assorted posters and portraits of family and friends.

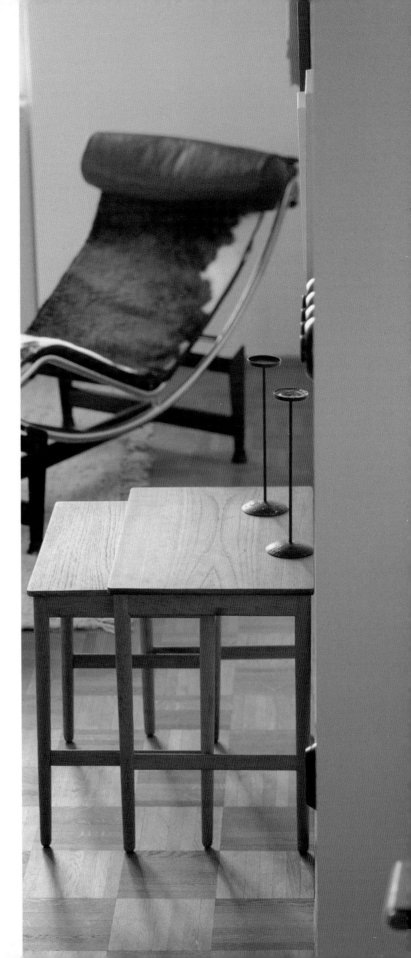

this page The open-plan kitchen is built from the Unoform system, designed by Danish architect Arne Munch in 1968. The long dining table with inbuilt candle holders was designed by Camilla Wessman. The spotlights, which are set into small brushed-steel boxes, are manufactured by the Belgian company Modular.

Hans Wegner. The ceilings are fitted with spotlights set into small brushed-steel boxes, made by the Belgian company Modular and offering an alternative to the ubitquitous recessed spotlights. All the doors in the apartment have inset rounded windows that are reminiscent of 1950s lift doors, and were designed by Wallensteen himself. The bathroom and kitchen feature several Danish design classics, including the sleek, elegant Vola series by Arne Jacobsen, the D-line series by Knud Holscher and the Unoform modular kitchen system, originally designed by Arne Munch in 1968.

Christer Wallensteen was responsible for overseeing the renovation of a Danish classic, the 1962 SAS (Scandinavian Airlines System) Haga Terminal building by Hack Kampmann, which is situated in the Haga royal park on the outskirts of Stockholm. It was used as a bus terminal and ticket office before falling into disuse, and had been empty for many years when Wallensteen was asked to renovate it. The Haga Terminal is now a restaurant and conference centre with an interior that sensitively respects the original structure while adding modern features. The same description could also be applied to Christer Wallensteen's own home.

below left Most doors in the apartment have rounded inset windows reminiscent of 1950s lift doors and were designed by Christer Wallensteen himself. The chair with a plastic string back is a cherished junk-shop find.

below The extra-long Vola tap/faucet was specially ordered so that it can be swivelled to fill both washbasin and bathtub.

Eero Aarnio

The Finnish designer Eero Aarnio is something of a maverick in the international design community, but one regarded with great respect. Aarnio's home reflects his personal design vision, but is also typical of an intellectual outlook on interiors that was particularly prevalent in Finland in the late 1960s.

Eero Aarnio has managed to put his trademark on both pure white and a spectrum of vibrant tones, drawing his design palette from all the colours of the rainbow. Aarnio's home, in the countryside at Veikkola, outside Helsinki, reflects his personal taste and is a showcase for his designs but the interior is also very characteristic of a more intellectual approach to interiors that gained popularity in Finland in the late 1960s.

For many people, the late 1960s were all about bold colours and groovy psychedelic patterns, but another movement was moving in quite the opposite direction.

above Aarnio designed the Screw table in 1991 to look ike a prop from a film where scientists have shrunk human beings to a fraction of their normal size. Playing with scale is very typical of his work.

right Surrounded by tall pine trees and with dense vegetation growing right up to the the house, the building is at one with nature.

opposite Two Bubble chairs float like soap bubbles. The see-through design is a reduction of Aarnio's original Ball chair. The chair is suspended from the ceiling to allow Aarnio to dispose of the base, something he wanted to achieve for aesthetic reasons. In the background is the Pastil chair, made from two fibreglass halves joined together.

After John Lennon met Yoko Ono and became involved with the experimental art scene, the two of them set up home in an all-white house, complete with white grand piano, white furniture and white walls. This shift from bold colour towards the purity of white is an often-forgotten side of the late 1960s, but at the time it was a refreshing and very radical contrast. The similarity to an art gallery interior is obvious, and the effect is to make the furniture look like part of an installation. This all-white style suits Finnish interiors particularly well, because Finnish design has always been reduced in form, and the use of white has been a recurring theme since the work of Alvar Aalto.

During the 1960s and 1970s, together with fellow Finns like Ristomatti Ratia, Yrjö Kukkapuro and Aarno Ruusuvuori, Aarnio introduced a new sense of modernity and sophistication to Finnish design and brought it to an international audience. His designs reveal his preoccupation with new materials and abstract rounded forms. The space-age Ball chair (1966) is a glossy sphere of moulded fibreglass that swivels on a steel base, while the Pastil is a curvaceous, abstract update of the rocking chair.

Aarnio's house is filled with prototypes, miniatures and different versions of his designs, including the celebrated Ball, Pony and Pastil chairs, showing that while many of his pieces are playful and quirky, they also work well in a more sophisticated interior, where their bold,

The house is filled with prototypes of Aarnio's own furniture, showing that while many of his pieces are playful and quirky, they also work well in a sophisticated interior.

abstract forms operate as sculpture just as much as furniture. The rigid moulded fibreglass forms of classic Aarnio pieces such as the Pastil chair may not look inviting at first glance, but its gentle curves cradle a seated body in a comforting fashion. Aarnio's designs provoke an immediate response. Their bold and curvy shapes, sly sense of humour and fantastical forms appeal to both young and old alike. With its strong visual impact, Aarnio's furniture has become something of a must-have for films, music videos and fashion shoots. The one thing it does require is space, but as Aarnio demonstrates in his own home, many of his pieces can still fit in next to a regular sofa.

opposite below Blinds are an effective way of dividing up the open floor plan without compromising the airy feel of the interior. The picture on the wall shows an outline of Aarnio's Pony chair.

this page A wall of bookshelves contrasts with the purity of the interior and shows that the house is a living home. Behind the Ball chair stands a row of miniatures of the chair, manufactured by the Vitra Design company. The Ball chair is a favourite prop for music-video and film producers.

this page and right The living room is washed with light from the huge windows. The glass coffee table is like an invisible shelf suspended in mid-air. The rocking chair (right) is one of Aarnio's most recent designs. The use of tubular steel is reminiscent of Bauhaus designs, but the chair has a playful appeal that is distinctively Aarnio.

below left and right Glass sculptures by Aarnio (left) and a glass lamp by Yki Nummi (right) are placed next to miniatures of the Pastil chair, which, just like the full-scale version, float if thrown into water.

Aarnio is a great Formula 1 fan and watches the races on television. His interest in Formula 1 lay behind his Formula chair of 1998, which was inspired by the success of Finnish driver Mika Häkkinen.

Due to the floor-to-ceiling glass windows, Aarnio's home is flooded with natural light all year round. When snow falls in winter and covers the vegetation outside in a thick blanket of white, it underlines the purity and simplicity of the interior. It might seem surprising that Aarnio used so much glass in the construction of his house, as he lives in a country that is covered by snow for at least a quarter of the year. Glass is not a good insulator of heat, but double glazing has been standard for generations in all Nordic countries, and many houses now have triple glazing. It keeps houses warm and snug and eliminates outside noise, although this is not a problem in a quiet location like that of the Aarnio house.

If any engine sounds are heard in the house, it is because Aarnio is a Formula 1 fan and enjoys watching the races on television, following the fortunes of Finnish driver Mika Häkkinen. His passion for Formula 1 was the inspiration for one of his designs: the Formula chair of 1998. This is a updated version of Aarnio's classic moulded fibreglass Pastil chair of 1968, but with a distinctive low-slung sports-car seat shape and a holder for a glass or beer can. The design is proof that Aarnio has a sense of humour but also a longevity in his design vision, despite changing trends. His house is a perfect testament to this vision.

right The warm and welcoming kitchen is at the heart of the house. Although open plan, it still retains elements of the traditional farmhouse kitchen, where friends and family gather round. Utensils, pots and pans are instantly accessible from the practical open shelves.

this page The sunken area is a feature Alvar Aalto used in many of his buildings, in particular libraries. Antti and Vuokko Nurmesniemi have employed the same concept but on a domestic scale. The furniture is all by Antti Nurmesniemi, including the custom-made sofa.

Antti and Vuokko Nurmesniemi

When two of the best-known designers in Finland built a home together, the result was always going to be spectacular. He was a product designer, she a textile designer, and together Antti and Vuokko Nurmesniemi both made their creative mark on their home.

When Antti and Vuokko Nurmesniemi designed and built their combined home and studio in 1975, they had already been married for 22 years. Quite independently of each other, they have been at the very forefront of Finnish design during the whole second half of the 20th century.

Vuokko Nurmesniemi (née Eskolin) studied at the School of Applied Art in Helsinki and joined the design studio of ceramics factory Arabia in 1952. She became Artistic Director at Marimekko at the tender age of twenty-three, long before the rest of the world had even heard of the company. At Marimekko she fused her knowledge of product design and functionalist thinking with fashion and came up with the Marimekko concept: easy-to-wear clothing, suitable for mass production, with a minimum of buttons, darts and other fussy details.

In 1953, Vuokko produced her stripy Piccolo textile design, later made up into Jokapoika (Every Boy) shirts, which became a standard uniform for American architects in the 1960s and are still in production today. While at

this page The Trienniale chair was designed by Antti Nurmesniemi in 1960, but only received its name after winning the Grand Prize at the Milan Trienniale in 1964, where Antti and Vuokko Nurmesniemi designed the Finnish stand. The chair is still in production by Piiroinen.

left On the stove stand two coffee pots by Antti Nurmesniemi dating from 1957. The design was commissioned by the Wärtsilä corporation because their large cast-iron factory did not have enough orders from the automobile industry to keep it busy at the time.

above Three levels in one room. The sleek, simple handrail is a masterpiece of reduction.

Marimekko, she also did a spell as designer at Nuutajärvi glassworks under Kaj Franck before leaving the textile company in 1960. In 1964 Vuokko Nurmesniemi started her own fashion house, Vuokko. Her bold pop-art clothing and international success won her great acclaim at home and abroad, and her designs have been described as 'garments in a class with industrial design'.

Antti Nurmesniemi enjoyed an equally long and celebrated career. His design work can be found everywhere in Finland, but perhaps his most Finnish

The Nurmesniemi home functions supremely well as a blueprint of the perfect live/work space, but perhaps this is hardly surprising, given the diverse and many talents of Antti and Vuokko Nurmesniemi.

product is also one of his earliest: the horseshoe-shaped sauna stool he designed for the Palace Hotel in 1951. It might be difficult to find a use for this beautiful stool outside a sauna, but it is nevertheless a design classic. Antti Nurmesniemi established his own design studio in 1956 and went on to work on products as diverse as coffee pots, furniture, graphics and high-voltage transmission towers. Along with Börje Rajalin, he was chief designer of the Helsinki metro trains. Nurmesniemi was also responsible for a wide variety of interiors, including the Finnish embassy in India. His designs are both very international and intensely Finnish, close to Italian and French post-modernism but always infused with Finnish functionality and colour. Antti Nurmesniemi won countless awards and titles, including that of professor and president of the ICSID (International Council of Societies of Industrial Design).

The Nurmesniemi home is the ultimate open-plan interior, thought out long before open-plan homes became a fashion statement. The industrial-looking ceiling framework gives it a distinctive appearance, and the ease with which different levels are combined is impressive. There is a sunken area in the main room that contrasts perfectly with a raised area right next to it, giving a bird's-eye view of three floors stacked in the same space without feeling cramped or crowded. Years ahead of its time, the Nurmesniemi home functions supremely well as the perfect live/work space, but perhaps this is hardly surprising given the many and diverse talents of Antti and Vuokko Nurmesniemi.

opposite In the foreground is a Deck Chair 001 and to the right are two Lounge Chairs 004, both of which are by Antti Nurmesniemi with upholstery by Vuokko Nurmesniemi.

right The work area of the house has generous storage cupboards and good lighting, pairing an oversized desk lamp with spotlights attached to the ceiling framework.

this page The Hockney sofa is by Eero Koivisto for David Design and the PK 22 chairs are by Poul Kjærholm. The oak units were designed by Eva Lilja Löwenhielm and Anya Sebton.

right An open staircase is reduced to its bare minimum.

Eva Lilja Löwenhielm

A 1966 semi-detached house in a leafy Stockholm suburb has been transformed by the designer Eva Lilja Löwenhielm to suit both her family and her work.

After leaving Beckmans design school in Stockholm in 1996, Eva Lilja Löwenhielm was awarded a scholarship by Swedish Elle Decoration and a prize for best new design by the Swedish Design Council. Producing work for both the Swedish furniture giant IKEA and many other smaller manufacturers allows Löwenhielm to vary her creative output. She works in many different materials – glass, wood, textiles and ceramics – and has created interiors for shops, homes and hotels. Her style is typical of good Scandinavian design: it is simple, beautiful and functional with a sense of humour, but it never screams for attention.

this page Wishbone chairs by Hans Wegner sit around the dining table. In front is a child's play area with Alvar Aalto stools.

opposite above Behind the dining table is a long sideboard storing crockery and glass.

opposite below The open-plan kitchen with its sleek units works well with the rest of the house.

The overall impression is that of order and structure but also comfort and ease of living – a harmonious combination of modern Swedish style and traditional Shaker interiors.

Her own home has offered a great opportunity for Eva Lilja Löwenhielm to try out new ideas and create the right setting for her own designs. Like many semi-detached houses built in Sweden during the 1960s, the structural quality and floor plan were excellent, but attention to detail was lacking. Eva Lilja Löwenhielm has stripped the house of all extraneous details: skirting boards, some internal doors and even the staircase handrail and used a simple palette of white, grey and natural oak. Great attention has been paid to creating good storage, which make it possible to conceal clutter and mess. With two children, this might sound like an impossible task, but in fact having fewer

Most of the furniture in the house consists of Scandinavian design classics from the middle of the last century.

items around makes life easier – there are fewer things to break and more space to play in. Most of the furniture in the house consists of Scandinavian design classics from the middle of the 20th century, including the PK 22 chair by Poul Kjærholm, the Wishbone chair by Hans Wegner, and the Ant and 3107 chairs by Arne Jacobsen. Other furniture includes the Hockney sofa and daybed by Eero Koivisto for the Swedish furniture company David Design. The floor is covered with hand-tufted wool rugs by Eva Lilja Löwenhielm for the IKEA designer collection PS.

The overall impression in this home is one of order and structure but also comfort and ease of living – a harmonious combination of modern Swedish style and traditional Shaker interiors. This look has become very popular in Sweden in the last few years, with architects like Jonas Lindvall and the trio Claesson Koivisto Rune acting as flagbearers. Eva Lilja Löwenhielm's home achieves this with large expanses of smooth white wall broken up by doors or openings with a minimal architectural framework. Untidy cables, ducts and pipes are all concealed and the oak floor meets the walls without any skirting boards.

The elegance and simplicity of of Eva Lilja Löwenhielm's home is deceptive – a look such as this may seem easily achievable but if you want to create this kind of effect, it is essential to have a builder who can appreciate the importance of the perfect finish.

above The studio has a row of white cabinets that offer generous storage space. Each desk has a classic chair: the Wishbone by Hans Wegner and the 3117 by Arne Jacobsen.

below right The bedroom is the simplest room, providing an atmosphere of calm tranquillity. The window offers views over the Baltic Sea.

above right The Hang Over chair by Finnish designer Vertti Kivi is suspended from the ceiling alongside the staircase. The rug was designed by Eva Lilja Löwenhielm for IKEA.

this page In a child's bedroom, a colourful Jungle puzzle designed by Pan Toivanen for the Finnish company Artek sits on top of the versatile cube storage unit. The bed is covered by a modern classic: a handwoven Cross throw by Pia Wallén. Only 100 throws are made each year on a wooden loom that dates back to the 19th century. On the floor is a wool rug designed by Eva Lilja Löwenhielm for IKEA.

Stockists and suppliers

The following retailers stock a selection of Scandinavian design:

UK

Abode

32 Kensington Gardens
Brighton BN1 4AL
01273 621116
www.abodeliving.co.uk
*Design House Stockholm,
iittala and Marimekko stockist*

Aria

Barnsbury Hall
Barnsbury Street
London N1 1PN
020 7704 6222
www.ariashop.co.uk
*Fritz Hansen, iittala and
Marimekko.*

Chaplins

477-507 Uxbridge Road
Hatch End, Pinner
Middlesex HA5 4JS
020 8421 1779
www.chaplins.co.uk
*Carl Hansen, Fritz Hansen,
Gubi, Kasthall and Swedese.*

The Conran Shop

81 Fulham Road
London SW3 6RD
020 7589 7401
www.conran.com
Also at Marylebone, London
and in Paris and Tokyo.
*Carl Hansen, Fritz Hansen
and Le Klint stockists.*

Fritz Hansen

13 Margaret Street
London W1W 8RN
020 7637 5534
www.fritzhansen.com
*The Republic of Fritz Hansen
store (operated by Skandium)
was the first dedicated Fritz
Hansen store in the world when
it opened in 2011. Besides
stocking the entire range of*

*this major manufacturer, it
also sells accessories, including
vintage glass and ceramics.*

Georg Jensen

15 New Bond Street
London W1S 3ST
020 7499 6541
www.georgjensen.com
*This Danish luxury provider
has been selling its classic
yet modern Scandinavian
homewares, watches and
jewellery on Bond Street
since 1921.*

The Granary

5 Bedford Street
Norwich NR2 1AL
01603 697107
www.jarrold.co.uk
*Part of the classic Norwich
department store group Jarrold,
The Granary is a stockist of
Design House Stockholm,
iittala and Marimekko.*

Heal's

196 Tottenham Court Road
London W1T 7LQ
020 7636 1666
www.heals.co.uk
*Ever since Sir Ambrose Heal
visited the Stockholm fair
in 1930, Heal's has been a
major stockist of modern
Scandinavian design, currently
focusing on Marimekko.*

The Home

Salt Mills
Victoria Road
Saltaire
Bradford BD18 3LB
01274 530770
www.thehomeonline.co.uk
*Artek, Carl Hansen, Fritz
Hansen, iittala and Georg
Jensen stockist located in very
nice surroundings for a day out.*

John Lewis

www.johnlewis.com
*Eva Solo, Georg Jensen, iittala,
Marimekko, Stelton and Secto.*

Marimekko

16–17 St Christopher's Place
London W1U 1NZ
020 7486 6454
www.marimekko.com
Britain's only Marimekko store.

Moleta Munro

4 Jeffrey Street
Edinburgh EH1 1DT
0131 557 4800
www.moletamunro.com
*Widest assortment of
Scandinavian design in Scotland.*

Nord

36 Bridge Street
Cambridge CB2 1UW
01223 321884
www.nordesign.co.uk
*Marimekko and iittala as well
as a café with a Scandinavian-
themed menu.*

SCP

135–139 Curtain Road
London EC2A 3BX
020 7739 1869
Visit their website for details
of their other store and
concessions at Selfridges in
London and Manchester
www.scp.co.uk
*Besides selling British and Italian
designs, SCP stocks Alvar Aalto
and Arne Jacobsen furniture
together with Poul Henningsen
and Verner Panton lighting. Also
some Scandinavian accessories.*

Shannon

68 Walcot Street
Bath BA1 5BD

01225 424222
www.shannon-uk.com
*Iittala, Marimekko and
anything Moomin, but also
most major Scandinavian
furniture and lighting brands.*

Skandium

245-249 Brompton Road
London SW3 2EP
020 7584 2066
www.skandium.com
and at
86 Marylebone High Street
London W1U 4QS
020 7935 2077
and
c/o Selfridges
400 Oxford Street
London W1A 1AB
020 7318 3379
*The single largest retailer of
original modern Scandinavian
design in Britain, representing
everyone who is anyone within
the field, be it in furniture,
lighting or accessories.*

Twentytwentyone

274 Upper Street
London N1 2UA
020 7288 1996
www.twentytwentyone.com
*20th-century design plus
the latest designs from
Scandinavia and beyond.*

Vessel

114 Kensington Park Road
London W11 2PW
020 7727 8001
www.vesselgallery.com
*Undoubtedly the best art
glass gallery in Britain, always
with a selection of unique
Scandinavian designs.*

US

ABC Carpet & Home
888 Broadway
New York, NY 10003
212 473-3000
www.abchome.com

Addo Novo
1313 Washington Street
Boston, MA 02118
857 284-7071
www.addonovo.com
Classic pieces by Arne Jacobsen, Poul Kjaerholm and Hans Wegner.

All Modern
www.allmodern.com
Iittala glassware, dinnerware and kitchenware, plus Le Klint shades, Verner Panton's Panthella lamp and a fine array of Panton's rug designs.

The Century House
3029 University Avenue
Madison, WI 53705
608 233-4488
www.centuryhouseinc.com
Modern Scandinavian interiors with furnishings from Swedese, Stokke and Carl Hansen.

Danish Design Store
www.danishdesignstore.com
Danish Modern furniture from Hans Wegner, Arne Jacobsen, Børge Mogensen and products from manufacturers including Louis Poulsen, Fredericia and Carl Hansen.

Design within Reach
Locations nationwide
www.dwr.com
Pieces by Eero Saarinen and Finn Juhl and lighting from Louis Poulsen.

Finnish Design Shop
www.finnishdesignshop.us
Over 70 Finnish brands, including Iittala, Arabia, Artek and Marimekko.

Form + Function
Nora Plaza
1300 E 86th Street
Indianapolis, IN 46240
317 569-9999
www.formplusfunction.net
Accessories from Marimekko and tableware from Stelton and Iittala.

Furniture from Scandinavia by Annette Rachlin
1531 33rd Street
Washington, DC. 20007
202 244-7876
www.furniturefromscandinavia.com
Classic pieces from leading Scandinavian manufacturers such as Woodnotes, Carl Hansen, Stelton, Fredericia and PP Møbler.

Georg Jensen
687 Madison Avenue
New York, NY 10021
212 759-6457
www.georgjensen.com
The US flagship store of this venerable brand was originally opened in 1924.

HIVE Modern
820 NW Glisan Street
Portland OR 97209
503 242-1967
www.hivemodern.com
Authorized dealers for Louis Poulsen and Le Klint lighting as well as Fritz Hansen and Carl Hansen furnishings, Eero Aarnio's designs and Iittala glass- and kitchenware.

Inform Interiors Seattle
300 Dexter Avenue North
Seattle, WA 98109
206 622-1608
www.informseattle.com
Alvar Aalto furniture from Artek as well as iconic pieces from Fritz Hansen and Carl Hansen.

Jules Seltzer
8833 Beverly Blvd
Los Angeles, CA 90048
310 274-7243
www.julesseltzer.com
A large selection of Toikka Birds from Iittala as well as furniture by Arne Jacobsen, Hans Wegner and Poul Kjaerholm.

Just Scandinavian
www.justscandinavian.com
Josef Frank's classic, celebrated textile designs as well as furniture by Finn Juhl and Asplund's Snow cabinets.

Luminaire
8950 NW 33rd Street
Miami, Florida 33172
305 437-7975
www.luminaire.com
Contemporary furniture and lighting design.

Morlen Sinoway Atelier
1052 West Fulton Market
Chicago, IL 60607
312 432-0100
www.morlensinoway.com
Designs by Alvar Aalto, Hans Wegner, Poul M. Vother and Poul Kjaerholm.

Scandinavian Grace
2866 State Route 28
Shokan, NY 12481
845 657-2759
www.scandinaviangrace.com
Classic and contemporary design from Scandinavia, including products from Asplund, Marimekko, Iittala and Kosta Boda.

Smart Furniture Inc.
430 Market Street
Chattanooga, TN 37402
888 467-6278
www.smartfurniture.com
Selection of classic Scandinavian Modern designs from Hans Wegner.

Stylus
1416 Ave Fernandez Juncos
San Juan
Puerto Rico 00909
787 501-5121
Carl Hansen furniture.

Suite NY
419 Park Avenue South
New York, NY 10016
212 421-3300
www.suiteny.com
Arne Jacobsen, Hans Wegner, Kaare Klint, Poul Kjaerholm and Ulla Koskinen.

Architects and designers

Whose work appears in this book:

Eero Aarnio
www.eero-aarnio.com
+358 9 25 68 547
Pages 2, 48, 49 r, 118–125

AEM Architects
80 O'Donnell Court
Brunswick Centre
Brunswick Square
London WC1N 1NX
+ 44 (0)20 7713 9191
Pages 50 l, 58–59

Galerie Mikael Andersen
Bredgade 63
DK-1260 Copenhagen
Denmark
+ 45 33 33 05 12
www.mikaelandersen.com
Pages 64–69

Asplund
(Showroom and store)
Sibyllegatan 31
SE-114 42 Stockholm
Sweden
+ 46 8 662 52 84
www.asplund.org
*Pages 3, 24–25, 33–34 a,
100–104*

Avanti Architects Limited
361–373 City Road
London EC1V 1AS
+ 44 (0)20 7278 3060
Page 56

Paul Daly Design Studio Ltd
11 Hoxton Square
London N1 6NU
+ 44 (0)20 7613 4855
www.pauldaly.com
Page 40 b

Nanna Ditzel MDD FCSD
Industrial designer specializing
in furniture, textiles, jewellery
and exhibitions
Nanna Ditzel Design
Trepkasgade 2
DK-2100 Copenhagen Ø
Denmark
+ 33 93 94 80
www.nanna-ditzel-design.dk
Pages 50 r, 52–53 l

Echo Design Agency
5 Sebastien Street
London EC1V OHD
+44 (0)20 7251 6990
Page 40 b

Johnson Naylor
13 Britton Street
London EC1M 5SX
+ 44 (0)20 7490 8885
www.johnsonnaylor.com
Pages 23 r, 40 ac

Finn Juhl Furniture
www.finnjuhl.com
*Pages 8, 9 r, 20 br, 21 a, 38 l,
38 br, 60, 82–87*

Kjærholm's
Rungstedvej 86
DK-2960 Rungsted Kyst
Denmark
+ 45 45 76 56 56
info@kjaerholms.dk
www.kjaerholms.dk
*Pages 7 main, 21 br, 22 l, 25 inset,
106–111*

Grethe Meyer Design
Valkendorfsgade 34
1151 Copenhagen K
Denmark
+ 45 33 12 26 87
www.grethemeyerdesign.com
*Pages 20 bl, 38–39 ar, 45 b,
70–75*

Modernity
Sibyllegatan 6
SE-114 31 Stockholm
Sweden
+ 46 8 20 80 25
www.modernity.se
*Pages 10, 12–13, 16 a, 16–17,
22–23, 41 r, 59 r*

**Studio Nurmesniemi/
Antti Nurmesniemi**
+ 358 9 684 7055
Construction: Paloheimo & Ollila,
Engineers
Heating, plumbing, air: Olavi
Pohjalaínen, engineer
Electricity: Risto Mäenpää,
engineer
Pages 36–37, 46 a, 126–131

Ratia Brand Co Oy
Kapteeninkatu 1 E
00140 Helsinki
Finland
+ 358 9 622 72820
ratia@ratia.com
www.ratia.com
Pages 4–5, 11, 26–27

Sanaksenaho Architects
Sepänkatu 15 C 45
00150 Helsinki
Finland
+ 358 9 177 341
www.kolumbus.fi/sanaksenaho
Pages 14–15, 88–93

Stelton AS
Christianshavns Kanal 4
DK-1406 Copenhagen K
Denmark
+ 45 39 62 30 55
www.stelton.dk
*Pages 44 inset, 45 a, 47 l, 55, 57,
62–63*

Jyrki Tasa, Architect
Arkkitehdit NRT Oy
Kalevankatu 31
00100 Helsinki
Finland
+ 358 9 686 6780
www.n-r-t.fi
Pages 6, 15 r, 29 r, 53 r

VX design & architecture
www.vxdesign.com
Page 51

**Wallensteen & Co ab
Architect and Design
Consultants**
Birger Jarlsg. 39
111 45 Stockholm
Sweden
+ 46 8 6115601
wallensteen@chello.se
Lighting: Konkret
Architects/Gerhard Rehm
Pages 112–117

Woodnotes OY
Tallberginkatu 1B
00180 Helsinki
Finland
+ 358 9694 2200
www.woodnotes.fi
*Pages 17 c, 17 r, 24 l, 34 b, 35,
76–81*

Picture credits

Photography by Andrew Wood (unless stated otherwise)   KEY: **a**=above, **b**=below, **r**=right, **l**=left, **c**=centre.

Endpapers Andrew Duncanson's (owner of Modernity) apartment in Stockholm, Sweden; **1** The Mogensen family's home in Gentofte, Denmark; **2** Eero Aarnio's house in Veikkola, Finland; **3** Michael Asplund's apartment in Stockholm, Sweden; **4-5** Ristomatti Ratia's apartment in Helsinki, Finland; **6** Into Tasa's house in Espoo, Finland, designed by architect Jyrki Tasa; **7 main** The Kjaerholms' family home in Rungsted, Denmark; **7 inset** A house in Stockholm, Sweden; **8 & 9 r** The Finn Juhl house, Charlottenlund, Denmark; **9 l** The Mogensen family's home in Gentofte, Denmark; **10** Andrew Duncanson's (owner of Modernity) apartment in Stockholm, Sweden; **11** Ristomatti Ratia's apartment in Helsinki, Finland; **12-13** Andrew Duncanson's (owner of Modernity) apartment in Stockholm, Sweden; **14-15** Matti and Pirjo Sanaksenaho's house in Espoo, Finland, designed by Sanaksenaho Architects; **15 r** Into Tasa's house in Espoo, Finland, designed by architect Jyrki Tasa; **16 a & 16-17** Andrew Duncanson's (owner of Modernity) apartment in Stockholm, Sweden; **16 b** A house in Stockholm, Sweden; **17 c & r** Mikko Puotila's apartment in Espoo, Finland. Interior design by Ulla Koskinen; **18-19** Coexistence, 020 7354 8817; **20 al** The Mogensen family's home in Gentofte, Denmark; **20 bl** Architect Grethe Meyer's house, Hørsholm, Denmark. Built by architects Moldenhawer, Hammer and Frederiksen, 1963; **20 ar** ph Thomas Stewart/Target Gallery, London; **20 br & 21a** The Finn Juhl house, Charlottenlund, Denmark; **21 bl** ph Thomas Stewart/Ice bucket and wooden bowl courtesy of Origin; **21 br-22 l** The Kjaerholms' family home in Rungsted, Denmark; **22-23** Andrew Duncanson's (owner of Modernity) apartment in Stockholm, Sweden; **23 r** Brian Johnson's apartment in London, designed by Johnson Naylor; **24 l** Mikko Puotila's apartment in Espoo, Finland. Interior design by Ulla Koskinen; **24-25** Michael Asplund's apartment in Stockholm, Sweden; **25 inset** The Kjaerholms' family home in Rungsted, Denmark; **26-27** Ristomatti Ratia's apartment in Helsinki, Finland; **28-29 & 29 l** ph Thomas Stewart/Target Gallery, London; **29 r** Into Tasa's house in Espoo, Finland, designed by architect Jyrki Tasa; **30 a** ph Thomas Stewart/Target Gallery, London; **30 b** ph Thomas Stewart/Glass courtesy of Skandium; **31** ph Thomas Stewart/Century London 020 7487 5100/Ceramic dishes courtesy of Gary Grant Choice Pieces; **32 & 33 inset** A house in Stockholm, Sweden; **33-34 a** Michael Asplund's apartment in Stockholm, Sweden; **34 b-35** Mikko Puotila's apartment in Espoo, Finland. Interior design by Ulla Koskinen; **36-37** Antti Nurmesniemi's house in Helsinki, Finland; **37 ar** ph Chris Everard/Ben Atfield's house in London; **37 br** ph Thomas Stewart; **38 l & 38 br** The Finn Juhl house, Charlottenlund, Denmark; **38-39 & 39 ar** Architect Grethe Meyer's house, Hørsholm, Denmark. Built by architects Moldenhawer, Hammer and Frederiksen, 1963; **39 background** ph Tham Nhu-Tran; **40 al** ph Thomas Stewart/Target Gallery, London; **40 ac** ph Tham Nhu-Tran/Brian Johnson's apartment in London, designed by Johnson Naylor; **40 b** ph Thomas Stewart/Yuen-Wei Chew's apartment in London designed by Paul Daly represented by

Echo Design Agency/White tableware courtesy of Rosenthal China; **40-41** ph Thomas Stewart/Target Gallery, London; **41 r** Andrew Duncanson's (owner of Modernity) apartment in Stockholm, Sweden; **42 l** ph Thomas Stewart/Century London 020 7487 5100/Dish courtesy of Gary Grant Choice Pieces; **42-43** ph Thomas Stewart/Tableware courtesy of Skandium; **43 r** ph Thomas Stewart/Century London 020 7487 5100; **44** A house in Stockholm, Sweden; **44 inset** & **45 a** Peter Holmblad's apartment in Klampenborg, Denmark, designed by architect Arne Jacobsen in 1958; **45 background** ph Tham Nhu-Tran; **45 b** Architect Grethe Meyer's house, Hørsholm, Denmark. Built by architects Moldenhawer, Hammer and Frederiksen, 1963; **46 a** Antti Nurmesniemi's house in Helsinki, Finland; **47 l** Peter Holmblad's apartment in Klampenborg, Denmark, designed by architect Arne Jacobsen in 1958; **47 r** A house in Stockholm, Sweden; **48 & 49 r** Eero Aarnio's house in Veikkola, Finland; **49 l** ph Thomas Stewart/Bowls courtesy of Skandium; **50 l** ph Chris Everard/a loft apartment in London designed by AEM Architects, lights courtesy of Skandium; **50 r** Nanna Ditzel's home in Copenhagen; **51** Ian Chee's apartment in London, chair courtesy of Vitra; **52-53 l** ph Nanna Ditzel's home in Copenhagen; **53 r** Into Tasa's house in Espoo, Finland, designed by architect Jyrki Tasa; **54 l** ph Chris Everard/Christina Wilson's house in London, lights courtesy of Century; **54 r** The Mogensen family's home in Gentofte, Denmark; **55** Peter Holmblad's apartment in Klampenborg, Denmark, designed by architect Arne Jacobsen in 1958; **56** ph Chris Everard/ Justin de Syllas & Annette Main's house in London, light courtesy of Skandium; **57** Peter Holmblad's apartment in Klampenborg, Denmark, designed by architect Arne Jacobsen in 1958; **58 l** ph Alan Williams/Director of design consultants Graven Images, Janice Kirkpatrick's apartment in Glasgow; **58–59** ph Chris Everard/a loft apartment in London designed by AEM Architects, lights courtesy of Skandium; **59 r** Andrew Duncanson's (owner of Modernity) apartment in Stockholm, Sweden; **60** The Finn Juhl house, Charlottenlund, Denmark; **61** ph Chris Everard/Christina Wilson's house in London; **62-63** Peter Holmblad's apartment in Klampenborg, Denmark, designed by architect Arne Jacobsen in 1958; **64-69** Gallery owner Mikael Andersen's studio house in Denmark, designed by Henning Larsen; **70-75** Architect Grethe Meyer's house, Hørsholm, Denmark. Built by architects Moldenhawer, Hammer and Frederiksen, 1963; **76-81** Mikko Puotila's apartment in Espoo, Finland. Interior design by Ulla Koskinen; **82-87** The Finn Juhl house, Charlottenlund, Denmark; **88-93** Matti and Pirjo Sanaksenaho's house in Espoo, Finland, designed by Sanaksenaho Architects; **94-99** The Mogensen family's home in Gentofte, Denmark; **100-104** Michael Asplund's apartment in Stockholm, Sweden; **106-111** The Kjaerholms' family home in Rungsted, Denmark; **112-117** Christer Wallensteen's apartment in Stockholm, Sweden; **118-125** Eero Aarnio's house in Veikkola, Finland; **126-131** Antti Nurmesniemi's house in Helsinki, Finland; **132-137** A house in Stockholm, Sweden.

Index

Page numbers in *italic* refer to captions and illustrations

ACKNOWLEDGMENTS

Magnus Englund and Chrystina Schmidt would like to thank Christopher Seidenfaden, Toby Anstruther and Solveig Bretag for believing in Skandium and thereby making this book possible, all our staff through the years, and all the location owners (past and present) who let us photograph their homes. Also hi to mum and dad!